1,000,000 Books

are available to read at

www.ForgottenBooks.com

Read online
Download PDF
Purchase in print

ISBN 978-1-330-75118-3
PIBN 10100644

This book is a reproduction of an important historical work. Forgotten Books uses state-of-the-art technology to digitally reconstruct the work, preserving the original format whilst repairing imperfections present in the aged copy. In rare cases, an imperfection in the original, such as a blemish or missing page, may be replicated in our edition. We do, however, repair the vast majority of imperfections successfully; any imperfections that remain are intentionally left to preserve the state of such historical works.

Forgotten Books is a registered trademark of FB &c Ltd.
Copyright © 2018 FB &c Ltd.
FB &c Ltd, Dalton House, 60 Windsor Avenue, London, SW19 2RR.
Company number 08720141. Registered in England and Wales.

For support please visit www.forgottenbooks.com

1 MONTH OF FREE READING

at
www.ForgottenBooks.com

By purchasing this book you are eligible for one month membership to ForgottenBooks.com, giving you unlimited access to our entire collection of over 1,000,000 titles via our web site and mobile apps.

To claim your free month visit:
www.forgottenbooks.com/free100644

* Offer is valid for 45 days from date of purchase. Terms and conditions apply.

English
Français
Deutsche
Italiano
Español
Português

www.forgottenbooks.com

Mythology Photography **Fiction**
Fishing Christianity **Art** Cooking
Essays Buddhism Freemasonry
Medicine **Biology** Music **Ancient Egypt** Evolution Carpentry Physics
Dance Geology **Mathematics** Fitness
Shakespeare **Folklore** Yoga Marketing
Confidence Immortality Biographies
Poetry **Psychology** Witchcraft
Electronics Chemistry History **Law**
Accounting **Philosophy** Anthropology
Alchemy Drama Quantum Mechanics
Atheism Sexual Health **Ancient History**
Entrepreneurship Languages Sport
Paleontology Needlework Islam
Metaphysics Investment Archaeology
Parenting Statistics Criminology
Motivational

SWEDENBORG:

HARBINGER OF THE NEW AGE
OF
THE CHRISTIAN CHURCH

BY

BENJAMIN WORCESTER

PHILADELPHIA
J. B. LIPPINCOTT COMPANY
1910

COPYRIGHT, 1910, BY HORACE PARKER CHANDLER AND
JAMES EVERETT YOUNG

ALL RIGHTS RESERVED

The natural man receiveth not the things of the Spirit of God, for they are foolishness unto him; neither can he know them, because they are spiritually discerned.
I Corinthians ii, 14.

Behold, I make all things new.
Revelation xxi, 5.

NOTE

THIS small work, while it may serve as a brief but compendious biography of the man Swedenborg, has the higher purpose to show how at the culmination of the desolation of the Church of our Lord, foretold by Him, He Himself by the orderly enlightening of the mind of one of His servants has provided for the enlightening of the many as to His Divine purpose and presence in His Holy Word — whereby His face may now again be seen in the clouds of the misinterpreted letter.

Those who desire more particulars about Swedenborg himself may find them in the author's "Life and Mission of Emanuel Swedenborg" (J. B. Lippincott Company), and in the three large volumes of Documents by R. L. Tafel (Swedenborg Society, London).

CONTENTS

I. The Consummation of the Age . . . 1

II. Emanuel Swedenborg: Parentage and Early Life 23

III. Scientific Pursuits at Home . . . 46

IV. Further Studies and Publications Abroad 75

V. Continued Study of the Body in Search of the Soul 106

VI. Continued Study of the Animal Kingdom: Spiritual Experience . 137

VII. Opening of Spiritual Sight: Unfolding of the Word 165

VIII. "The Apocalypse Explained" and Other Works 189

IX. Manner of Life in Later Period . 209

X. Later Period of Life: Conclusion . 249

Index 287

SWEDENBORG

HARBINGER OF THE NEW AGE

I

THE CONSUMMATION OF THE AGE

THE Christian Church recognizes that it is entering upon a new stage of life, with promise of a freer, more spiritual, and more beneficent existence than it has yet known. Of the immediate cause of this new development, and of its place in fulfilment of the predictions of our Lord, the Church at large has little or nothing to say. Only in the inner content of these predictions, as unfolded by Swedenborg, is the light now breaking from the east even unto the west plainly seen to be that of the Lord's Second Coming, with His Holy Spirit, calling all things to our remembrance whatsoever He has said unto us and guiding us into all truth. For clearer apprehension of this epoch in men's spiritual development let us take a rapid glance, approximately from Swedenborg's own point of view, over the course of this development from its inception.

Our highest conception of the Creator is of Infinite Love, Infinite Wisdom, Infinite Power. Man's creation into the Divine image and likeness means therefore the form and capacity with which he is endowed to receive and live his measure of this Love, Wisdom, and Power. For the basis of his existence he has a material, animal nature, with its instincts and inflow of life from the Only Life. For development into the image and likeness of the Creator he has an inner organism, consisting of heart to receive and give forth love and of understanding to receive and utter wisdom, with liberty and power to act therefrom. The handmaid of the understanding is observation, the master of the house is reason — the power of collating ideas and drawing conclusions. To the handmaid the universe unfolds itself in which as in a mirror may be seen the Divine purpose, creating an infinity of organisms for mutual ever-ascending service, with man himself at the head, anointed with the high mission to aspire to the Divine image, and to accept the Divine will for his own. But the fulfilling of this

THE CONSUMMATION OF THE AGE

mission depends on his accepting with heart and reason the Divine guidance, which at all times and under all conditions is provided in such form as can be in freedom accepted — in the "still small voice," in inspired words, or in portentous signs.

It is the accumulation of these revealings of the Divine will that has come down to us in our Holy Scriptures, in which we recognize the Purpose or Word of God in adaptation to the various states and conditions of men. This Word, or revelation of the Divine will, is given in man's own language and form of thought, even as our Lord Himself gave it to the people in parable. But in coming forth through heaven into man's thought and speech, the Word does not lose its Divine content. It simply embodies this in corresponding forms of lower degree. Thus this written Word is the foot of a ladder on which man and angel may ascend in thought into the presence of its Giver. Under this recognition of the spiritual and Divine content of the Scriptures incongruities in the letter are easily referable to human crudities of thought. Within, all is compatible with the infinite wisdom and love of Him whose will it reveals, full of instruction for angels and men.

EMANUEL SWEDENBORG

The first chapter of the Book of Genesis sets forth in terms a child may in his manner apprehend the order of the Divine process of creation. Of this order the first element is the outgoing of the Divine life through successive degrees of spiritual and material substance that it creates, of less and less, even to least life. *In the beginning God created the heaven and the earth.* In the outmost, least living substance created there is yet a certain power of reaction, born of its very inertness. And the second element of the Divine order of creation is that out of this first, simple, least-living recipient through its reaction are evolved by regular — we say natural — process higher, more complex, and more living recipients, to receive higher or inner degrees of life from the One Source. The third element of this order is that this advance is made stage by stage, day after day, evening being the womb of the new morning. *Evening was and morning was one day.* This involves the decline of each successive stage after serving its purpose and maturing the germ for a new stage. Thus one generation of life gives way to its successor. The corn of wheat falls to the ground and dies in bringing forth a new

THE CONSUMMATION OF THE AGE

plant, in which in new form its life is continued. The leaf falls after having formed in its axil the bud for a new shoot, and in decaying furnishes food for the new growth. Last in order, we learn that man in the image and likeness of his Creator is the first and final purpose in all creation.

How beautifully this order was followed in the creation of the earth and its inhabitants is known to the geologist, even as summarized in the record of Genesis up to the first presentation of man in the Divine image and likeness. And a deeper, higher fulfilment of the same order is found by Swedenborg in the evolution of the spiritual man into this image and likeness, out of the mind formless and void of the mere animal man — represented by the formless and empty earth enshrouded in darkness. And again in the same record is found the order of evolution of the spiritual man out of the natural to all time.

Of the primeval man we can know little. He left no records, no tradition. Of the regenerated heavenly but infantile race represented by Adam and Eve, first reproducing in infantile manner the Divine image and implanting in the inmost consciousness of mankind a foregleam of the condi-

EMANUEL SWEDENBORG

tion to which it should in the end attain, Swedenborg learned much in the other world, quite in accordance with our traditions of the Golden Age. With this called by him the Most Ancient Church the history of man begins, though in scarce other than mythical form. Of the immediate revelation to it of the Divine will we have intimation in the voice of the Lord God heard by Adam. Of its duration we know nothing, but may conjecture it to have equalled all recorded time. Of its decline, due to the growing child desire to taste and choose for himself what to call good, we have symbolized record in the following of the serpent's counsel and in the decadent generations of Adam. The moral and spiritual desolation at the end of this first church swamped by accumulating falsities is represented by the flood, out of which was Divinely rescued the germ for a new development under the name of Noah [Rest].

The men of this succeeding age, called by Swedenborg the Ancient Church, though no longer to be led by the angels of infancy who do always behold the face of the Father in heaven, were yet willing to be instructed of heaven through their wise men learned in ancient tradi-

THE CONSUMMATION OF THE AGE

tions. With growing power of thought and imagination their successive generations developed language, song, and art — notably that of building — during thousands or myriads of years, over all central and southwestern Asia and northeastern Africa. Of their religion, at first heaven-derived and spiritual, we have remains in the early Hebrew Scriptures and in the sacred books of India, Persia, Egypt, and Turkestan. On the remains of their language all our modern languages are based. Of their prowess in building, the rock-temples of India and the pyramids of Egypt bear enduring witness, though of the period of religious decadence. Of their art the remains left in Greece by a late offshoot of the same stock, are still unequalled by modern genius. Grecian art and philosophy with Roman statesmanship have furnished the basis of modern civilization, as the Gospel of our Lord has furnished the inspiration — even as we see exemplified in the evolution of the heaven-aspiring Christian cathedral.

In the discriminating thought of this Ancient Church at its best estate it distinguished and reverenced divers attributes of the Deity. In its de-

EMANUEL SWEDENBORG

cadence these attributes were personified and imaged, till in its downfall the images themselves were worshipped and idolatry was becoming universal. Then lest the knowledge of the One God and of His laws of life should be lost from the face of the earth, midway in both time and space between the erection of the pyramids and that of the Grecian temples, in the very centre of civilization, a new race was planted, in the land of Canaan — the old home perhaps of Adam and Eve — a race of Shemitic, still Noachian stock, a simple, nomadic race of unequalled persistence, fitting them to receive and preserve in integrity a new revelation of the Creator and His laws in concrete form — even graven in stone. These laws accompanied by many ritual statutes, with remains of the earlier Scriptural records, with the true yet symbolic history of this people, with their songs of prayer and praise, with prophecy from beginning to end of the coming of the Messiah who should bring dire judgment on their nation for their sins while bringing eternal salvation to those who would accept His redemption — all this was the spiritual legacy of this Noachian age to the ages to come. Says Schlegel —

THE CONSUMMATION OF THE AGE

"The significant brevity of the first pages of the Mosaic history involves much profound truth for us in these later ages . . . did we but know how to extract the simple sense with like simplicity. . . . In general the whole tenor of the Mosaic writings, like the existence of the Hebrew nation, was formed for futurity. . . . So the whole Hebrew people may in a lofty sense be called prophetic, and have been really so in their historical existence and destiny."[1] "The Hebrew tongue was eminently adapted to the high spiritual destination of the Hebrew people, and was a fit organ of the prophetic revelation and promises imparted to that nation."[2]

The ever deplorable conduct of the Jewish leaders in crucifying Him who came to save them ended the leadership of that church in the spiritual development of mankind. But their traditions, their Scriptures remained to become the framework of the new church of the Lord, itself the prototype of the New Jerusalem, His final tabernacle with men. And we are never to forget the maternal service of the Hebrew Church for the birth of its Lord into the world, first in the written

[1] *Philosophy of History*, p. 120.   [2] *Ib.* p. 250.

EMANUEL SWEDENBORG

Word and then in its fulfilment in the flesh, our ever present Lord. The maternal office was not more real materially than it was spiritually. It was foretold to Eve with reference to her seed. It was repeated to Abraham who rejoiced to see the day coming. Its fulfilment was the theme of the prophets and was voiced in the Psalms of David. Abraham's obedience, repeated in Mary's *Behold the handmaid of the Lord: be it unto me as thou hast said*, furnished the fit germ for the human life of our Lord. And Mary said, *My soul doth magnify the Lord, and my spirit hath rejoiced in God, my Saviour.*

Our Lord's coming in the flesh bringing the light of the Divine presence down among men caused a judgment on those to whom the light came, both in this world and in the world of spirits where the evil were assaulting the gates of heaven itself. His resistance to their assault upon His human nature at the same time cast them down in the spirit world to their home beneath, even as He declared — *I beheld Satan as lightning fallen from heaven*. But the Lord came not merely for judgment. He came also for a light to enlighten the Gentiles. The Gentiles were all people out-

THE CONSUMMATION OF THE AGE

side of the Jewish race. And indeed it was among these outside nations that His light was chiefly accepted and His Church established, on the faith that He was the Christ, the Son of the living God. In Him at last was seen Man in the image and likeness of God. He first did the will of the Father on earth as it is done in heaven, therein giving man the example for all time, abiding in him and by His Holy Spirit giving him the will to follow, as he will receive it. The world was ripe for the beginning of this realization of what living in the image and likeness of God might mean, as is evident from its marvellous spread during the early centuries; but only for the beginning. The young man thought he desired eternal life, the life of the kingdom of heaven. But when told to renounce all that he had of this world, he was very sorrowful, for he had great possessions. It was not difficult for the first disciples to give up worldly possessions, of which they had no great store — to forsake their nets and follow their Lord. But for this they at once asked what reward they should have in heaven, and disputed among themselves which should there be the greatest. Doubtless in this claim for reward in His kingdom the Lord saw the tares sown with the wheat and foresaw the sad end of this first age of His Church. None knew so well as He the slow and painful steps by which man must be led out of the natural self-seeking life of this world into the spiritual self-devoting life of the Father's kingdom.

Man was yet but in early youth. A great step was gained in teaching him to set his heart, not on the riches and honors of earth where moth and rust doth corrupt, but on the treasures in heaven where neither moth nor rust doth corrupt and thieves do not break through nor steal. The tares must be let alone until a riper age, when their fruit should be manifest and the developed reason should be ready to bind them in bundles and burn them. But this acceptance of the Gospel mainly through fear of torment or hope of reward in heaven gave every opportunity to self-seeking leaders for gaining control of their converts to their own personal advantage. Retaining the Gospel in their own hands, in a language which none but themselves could read, they devised creeds and canons to maintain their own supremacy. They took away the key of

THE CONSUMMATION OF THE AGE

knowledge. Entering not into the kingdom themselves, them that would enter they hindered, all to their own worldly gain.

Luther and his associates revolted from this prostitution of the religion of our Lord, so graphically represented to John in vision as Babylon the great adulteress. And in two centuries they and their followers did much to restore a true conception of the life of the kingdom and of the duty of the Church. But in controverting the error that heaven could be merited by undergoing the penances and paying the tribute imposed by the Church of Rome, substituting therefor belief only in the saving grace of Jesus Christ, Luther went too far. To emphasize the distinction between his Reformed Church and the Roman Catholic, he declared charity and good works to be of no avail for salvation.

In the Protestant wing of the Church belief in the vicarious sacrifice of Jesus Christ was the only means of attaining heaven, and the condemnation of all who had not this grace was proclaimed with a severity equal to that of the anathemas of the Church of Rome. Either wing of the Lord's Church was ready to burn the other. The errors of both were sustained by a fundamental misunderstanding of the Trinity, which was unfortunately conceived as of distinct persons with different attributes. The Father was regarded as avenging justice and the Son as loving mercy, by which He atoned for the never-forgiven sin of Adam in taking upon Himself the punishment of the cross, the Father accepting the sacrifice so far as to pardon those whom the Son should elect.

Thus darkened was the Sun of heaven. This unreasonableness of doctrine and lack of Christian charity, wars and massacres under the flag of Christian faith, with the profligate luxury of church officials in contrast with the desperate poverty of the people, easily bred contempt for religion at a time when by the art of printing great strides had been made in popular education. What wonder that atheism and deism were having their own way! Religion and morality in the eighteenth century were fast disappearing. The judgment of the Christian Church in the view of its sanest adherents was near at hand.

John Albert Bengel [d. 1752] said, " The doctrine of the Holy Spirit is already gone; that of

THE CONSUMMATION OF THE AGE

Christ is on the wane; and that of the creation hangs but by a slender thread. . . . It is made a part of politics so to act and speak as to leave no trace of religion, God, and Christ." [1]

Dr. Dörner says, "The edifice of Lutheran Christology had been for the most part already forsaken by its inhabitants before 1750. . . . A deistical atmosphere seemed to have settled upon this generation, and to have cut it off from vital communion with God." [2]

Leibnitz in the earlier part of the century had said, "The state to which we are approaching is one of the signs by which will be recognized that final war announced by Jesus Christ: *Nevertheless, when the Son of Man cometh, shall He find faith on the earth?*" [3]

Abbey and Overton say, "It was about the middle of the century when irreligion and immorality reached their climax." [4]

In 1753 Sir John Barnard said, "At present it really seems to be the fashion for a man to de-

---

[1] Dr. J. S. Dörner: *Hist. Prot. Theology*, ii, 213.
[2] *Ib.* ii, 274, 296.
[3] Palmer: *The Church of Christ*, i, 348.
[4] *English Church in Eighteenth Century*, ii, 44.

clare himself of no religion." And Archbishop Lecker declared that immorality and irreligion were grown almost beyond ecclesiastical power.[1]

In France it was if possible worse, and Carlyle well says, " A century so opulent in accumulated falsities . . . opulent in that bad way as never century before was! Which had no longer the consciousness of being false, so false had it grown; and was so steeped in falsity, and impregnated with it to the very bone, that—in fact the measure of the thing was full, and a French Revolution had to end it." [2]

"In Germany," says Schlegel, "during the atheistic and revolutionary period of the French philosophy, immediately prior to the French Revolution, as well as at its commencement, Christianity and in fact all religion was regarded as a mere prejudice of the infancy of the human mind, totally destitute of foundation in truth, and no longer adapted to the spirit of the age; monarchy and the whole civilization of modern Europe as abuses no longer to be tolerated. It was only when men had reached this extreme term of their

---

[1] ABBEY AND OVERTON: *op. cit.* ii, 44.
[2] *Life of Frederick the Great*, i, 11.

THE CONSUMMATION OF THE AGE

boasted enlightenment, that a reaction took place. But prior to this, toward the middle of the eighteenth century, and in the ten years immediately subsequent, the spirit of the age bore all before it in its irresistible progress." [1]

This condition of the Christian Church in the eighteenth century was plainly the abomination of desolation foretold by the Lord as to come at the consummation of the age [commonly but erroneously rendered "the end of the world"], when the Sun — the face of the Lord of heaven — should be darkened, and the Moon — faith in Him — should not give her light, and the stars of heaven — all knowledge of Him and His will — should fall from their places. Such it was recognized to be by devout, distressed students of the time, and the judgment foretold by our Lord and foreseen in vision by John was perceived to be at hand. By concurrent testimony it would seem that the time was ripe for this judgment in the middle of the eighteenth century. The judgment was not seen to come. But notably from about that time a change came over the Christian Church, and students of history ever since are

[1] *Op. cit.* ii, 268.

17

EMANUEL SWEDENBORG

marvelling, searching for the cause of the revivification of the churches. A downward course does not of itself turn into an upward course. Satan does not let go his hold of man or race of his own will. As in the first century, so in the eighteenth, he could be cast down from his encroachment on heaven by no less power than that of the Son of God, the Word made flesh and dwelling among us.

It was the sign of the Son of Man to be seen again in the clouds of heaven that was to effect the judgment. It was the Lion of the tribe of Judah who alone could prevail to loose the seals of the Book, at once the Book of the Word and the Book of the judgment. The two prophecies are one. In the written Word after the resurrection, as in the flesh transfigured on the mount, the Lord showed Himself to His disciples in glory, Son of God in Son of Man. But in the succeeding centuries, as we have seen, clouds of misinterpretation, the clouds of tri-personalism, of vicarious atonement, and of salvation by faith alone, had hidden His face from men's minds. The dispersion of these clouds, the re-appearance of the face — the grace and truth — of the Son of **Man**, even

THE CONSUMMATION OF THE AGE

in the letter of His written Word, was to effect the judgment on the declining age of the Church and reveal the dawning light of the new age.

Under this simple interpretation of the judgment we are to look for its effects in the clearing of the spiritual atmosphere, in release of men's minds from the bondage of perverted faith — Peter girded by another and carried whither he would not — and in increasing return to the simple, heart-felt instruction of the Gospel. It was the beloved disciple John who was to remain till his Lord should come again, and to whom in vision the spiritual judgment was portrayed — John, who stands for the love of the Church in good works, as Peter for its faith. And as among the Jews at our Lord's first coming, so in the midst of the desolation of the eighteenth century there were not a few memorable examples of God-fearing, self-denying, Samaritan lives. Into this good heart coupled with trained intellect, preserved as the germ for the new age, was received the first dawn of light, and in the marvellous spread of this light thus far we recognize the certainty of the Lord's renewed presence in His Church. Most strikingly is this shown in the

EMANUEL SWEDENBORG

new charity now prevailing between one sect of the Church and another and between Christian and pagan. Never before since the angels' song was heard on the hills of Judea — Peace on earth and good-will toward men — has its accomplishment seemed so near. Year by year, day by day is the evidence accumulating that the crisis is past and the new coming of our Lord begun, and this dating from about the middle of the eighteenth century. But where and how was the vision to John fulfilled?

No one answers but Swedenborg, who in his *Apocalypsis Revelata* describes the fulfilment, clause by clause, of the whole of this vision — not in this world, but in the vast spirit world, where were gathered an innumerable multitude, good and bad together, awaiting the judgment that the new coming of the Lord in His Word would effect. Were this conception of the judgment mere imagination, instead of the stern reality which Swedenborg affirms, how sublime! Judgment of scores of generations in place of the one or two possible on earth, without limit of space or time; judgment of the inner souls and tenets of men there revealed; overthrow of spirit

THE CONSUMMATION OF THE AGE

heavens and earth, leaving this earth of ours to bide its time; angels without number bearing the Divine light down to the overthrow of the prince of darkness and all his satellites! In truth the spirit world alone could be fit theatre for the fulfilment of the vision vouchsafed to John. But on earth the seals of the Book were to be loosed at the same time, for spirits in the flesh live always in real though unseen communion with spirits in the spirit world, and their thoughts are held in common. In fact, with spirits as with men, spiritual thought must have its ultimate basis in material thought. The letter of the Word of God is human, even material, in form. The opening of its inner, spiritual, heavenly, and Divine content can be only by the Lord Himself by means of His Holy Spirit in the suitably prepared mind of man.

Before He left their sight the Lord told His disciples that He had many things to say to them, but they could not bear them then. Howbeit when He should come to them with His Holy Spirit He would call all things to their remembrance whatsoever He had said unto them and would guide them into all truth. A special fulfilment of this promise was given to these immediate disciples,

EMANUEL SWEDENBORG

for their special vocation, but its larger, all-embracing fulfilment could not come till the new revelation of His face in His Word, which was indeed the same thing, and before which the Gospel must first be preached unto all the nations. It was by the opening of the heart to the Holy Spirit that the revelation of the grace and truth in His Word could be given.

The Word from Alpha to Omega is one. Only the interpretation varies as gradually given with man's developing capacity to receive. The ages for infantile reception, for childhood instruction and obedience, for blind reliance on priests and their dogmas, had passed. The new light now needed must explain the will of God and His providence for man in a rational, intelligible way, not as a substitute for faith, but as her handmaid, for her ultimate support. It must be addressed to the understanding and must therefore come, not with authority to compel, but with light leading into all truth, in accordance with our Lord's promise. The mind to receive this new light in fulness must be trained in the learning and reason of the world, and the heart must be open to the Spirit. Where was it to be found?

II

EMANUEL SWEDENBORG: PARENTAGE AND EARLY LIFE

IN the middle of the seventeenth century was living an honest, God-fearing, and prosperous miner named Daniel Isaksson, with his wife Anna, daughter of a Swedish pastor, on his homestead called Sweden, a hundred and twenty miles northwest from Stockholm. Grateful for the large family Heaven sent them, Daniel would often say at dinner, "Thank you, my children, for this meal, for I have dined with you and not you with me: God has given me food for your sakes." His second son Jesper, born in 1653, took the name Swedberg from the homestead. Later, when for his services to church and state his family was ennobled, Jesper's children received the name Swedenborg, though the father himself retained the name Swedberg. Inheriting his father's piety, on being rescued in boyhood from imminent death — caught under a mill-wheel — he resolved never to forget either morning or evening to commit

EMANUEL SWEDENBORG

himself to God's keeping and to the protection of His holy angels.

Having received an excellent education at Upsal and abroad, in 1685 Jesper Swedberg was ordained and appointed first chaplain to the King's regiment of Life Guards, later royal chaplain at Stockholm. To the soldiers he taught the catechism and to King Charles XI he preached boldly without fear or favor, yet so pleasing the King that their Majesties stood as godfather and godmother to one of his daughters. "Ask of me," said the King, "what you will and you shall have it." But Swedberg, as he says, never asked the least thing for himself or his family, using his influence only for the appointment of faithful men to office. For a time he was the beloved pastor of a small parish, then on the King's insistence became Professor, and afterward Rector of the University at Upsal. By the King's orders he prepared and published, largely at his own expense, a revision of the Swedish Bible, which was however suppressed by the jealousy of the clergy. At Upsal where Emanuel passed his childhood Swedberg during several professorships and as Dean of the cathedral devoted himself to the well-being

PARENTAGE AND EARLY LIFE

of the students, and so successfully that he was constantly cheered by their affection, and he could say after his ten years' life with them that in all that time the King had never received a single bad report of them.

In 1703 this pleasant life at Upsal was interrupted, to Swedberg's entire surprise, by his receiving from the young King Charles XII an appointment as Bishop of Skara, whither he then removed and settled at Brunsbo. He was now fifty years old, and here he remained till his death at eighty-two, never until the last few years neglecting to officiate in public worship. He preached indefatigably from the Gospels and the Epistles, his sermons always flowing without any straining from the text; for, said he, " then God recognizes His own Word." But though always making the duties of his sacred office his chief care, the good bishop was a devoted husband and father. He had married in 1683 Sara Behm, of good family, her father long holding the same office later held by her son Emanuel, that of Assessor in the College of Mines. By a previous marriage to the then Dean of Upsal she had inherited a considerable fortune, which later proved of great assistance in the support of Bishop Swedberg's family and in his numerous publications.

Jesper and Sara's first child was a son who died in his twelfth year. Asked by his father what he should do in heaven, he answered, "I shall pray for my father and brothers and sisters." The second child was Anna, to whom and to her husband Ericus Benzelius — in 1742 made Archbishop of Sweden — Emanuel was always tenderly attached. He was the next child, born January 29, 1688, while his father was serving as royal chaplain at Stockholm. Of the name given him his father wrote in his autobiography, "I am fully convinced that children ought to be given such names as will awaken in them and call to their minds the fear of God and everything that is orderly and righteous. . . . The name of my son Emanuel signifies God-with-us — that he may always remember God's presence, and that intimate, holy, and mysterious conjunction with our good and gracious God into which we are brought by faith, by which we are conjoined with Him and are in Him. And blessed be the Lord's name! God has to this hour been with him.

PARENTAGE AND EARLY LIFE

And may He be further with him until he be eternally united with Him in His kingdom! . . . I am a Sunday child; and the mother of my children, my late wife, was also a Sunday child, and all my children were Sunday children except Catharine, who was born at Upsal on the third day of Easter." After Emanuel came six sons and daughters, the last being Margaretha, born in 1695, their good mother dying the following year, when Emanuel was nine years old.

It was in 1719 that the family was ennobled by Queen Ulrica Eleonora with the name of Swedenborg, and Benzelius with the name of Benzelstierna, after which they were entitled to seats in the Diet. The Bishop, however, worked quietly on under his old name till his death in 1735, preaching, writing, and publishing without ceasing, though with small encouragement and few sales. Of his numerous publications he said, "If I had all the money which I have invested in the printing of books, I would be worth now from sixty to seventy thousand dalers in copper." These were largely sermons and other religious works, but also books on the Swedish language, grammar and lexicons, school-books,

EMANUEL SWEDENBORG

his new Swedish Bible, and a commentary. His autobiography is preserved which he wrote for his children, and he had much correspondence with the colonial missions, especially that of Pennsylvania and Delaware. This mission had been established by his influence with the King and had elected Swedberg their first bishop, as had also the Swedish churches at London and Lisbon, with the King's sanction.

With these functions and labors of the father we are concerned only as they throw light on the character and ability transmitted to the son. We learn his piety, his faith manifested in charity and good works, his loving zeal in the cares intrusted to him, his learning, his integrity and boldness for the right, and his indefatigable industry. All these traits were indispensable for the discharge of the mission to be intrusted to the son. And another characteristic, less common with other races, he held from his Scandinavian ancestry, of utmost importance to the son — his constant sense of Divine and angelic supervision of the affairs of men. In his first year at Upsal Jesper had such a wonderful dream that he did not know whether he ought not to call it a reve-

PARENTAGE AND EARLY LIFE

lation. He said, "No human tongue can pronounce and no angel can describe what I then saw and heard." He firmly believed that "God's angels are especially present in this sacred office [of Divine worship]." He felt sure that he was specially protected by angels from malign influences and directed in his studies at the University. How essential was this trust and confidence in Divine and heavenly influences to the service in store for his son Emanuel we shall see as we go on.

Of Emanuel's childhood he himself wrote late in life in answer to the inquiries of his friend Dr. Beyer, "From my fourth to my tenth year I was constantly engaged in thought upon God, salvation, and the spiritual experiences of men; and several times I revealed things at which my father and mother marvelled, saying that angels must be speaking through me. From my sixth to my twelfth year I used to delight in conversing with clergymen about faith, saying that the life of faith is love, and that the love which imparts life is love to the neighbor; also that God gives faith to every one, but that those only receive it who practise that love." Thus early was he imbued, doubtless by his father, with what remained the contention of his life. Born in Stockholm, removed with his father to Upsal when four years old, he received there his education as a schoolboy and later as a student in the University. His thesis at the conclusion of his course was a series of selections from Greek and Latin authors, together with some from Scripture, presenting certain moral and religious sentiments accompanied with apposite reflections, indicating his trend of thought at that time of life. Little more is known of his life at the University, but he was doubtless living with his sister Anna and Benzelius, his father having removed to his bishopric. From his letters to these much loved friends we learn what we know of his next ten years of study pursued mostly abroad. Within a few months after leaving the University he wrote from his father's home at Brunsbo begging of Benzelius letters to some English college, that he might there improve himself in mathematics, or in physics and natural history. He adds to his request —

"As I have always desired to turn to some practical use and also to perfect myself in the studies which I selected with your advice and ap-

PARENTAGE AND EARLY LIFE

proval, I thought it advisable to choose a subject early which I might elaborate in course of time, and into which I might introduce much of what I should notice and read in foreign countries. This course I have always pursued hitherto in my reading; and now at my departure I propose to myself, as far as concerns mathematics, gradually to gather and work up a certain collection, namely, of things discovered and to be discovered in mathematics — or, what is nearly the same thing, the progress made in mathematics during the last one or two centuries." "Much kind love" he sends to his sister Anna.

While awaiting letters, the royal permission, and perhaps money for his expenses, the young graduate learns the art of bookbinding and practises music, occasionally filling the organist's place at church. At length in 1710, the permission having been obtained by his father, he sets out for London, whence in October he writes to Benzelius —

"This island has also men of the greatest experience in this [mathematical] science; but these I have not yet consulted, because I am not yet sufficiently acquainted with their language. I study

EMANUEL SWEDENBORG

Newton daily, and I am very anxious to see and hear him. I have provided myself with a small stock of books for the study of mathematics, and also with a certain number of instruments. . . . The magnificent St. Paul's Cathedral was finished a few days ago in all its parts. . . . The town is distracted by internal dissensions between the Anglican and Presbyterian churches; they are incensed against each other with almost deadly hatred. . . . Were you, dear brother, to ask me about myself, I should say I know that I am alive, but not happy; for I miss you and my home. . . . I not only love you more than my own brothers, but I even love and revere you as a father. . . . May God preserve you alive, that I may meet you again!"

Again he writes in the following April — "I visit daily the best mathematicians here in town. I have been with Flamsteed, who is regarded the best astronomer in England, and who is constantly taking observations, which, together with the Paris observations, will give us some day a correct theory respecting the motion of the moon and of its appulse to fixed stars. . . . Newton has laid a good foundation for correcting the irregularities

PARENTAGE AND EARLY LIFE

of the moon in his *Principia*. ... You encourage me to go on with my studies; but I think that I ought rather to be discouraged, as I have such an 'immoderate desire' for them, especially for astronomy and mechanics. I also turn my lodgings to some use, and change them often. At first I was at a watchmaker's, afterward at a cabinet-maker's, and now I am at a mathematical-instrument maker's. From them I learn their trades, which some day will be of use to me. I have recently computed for my own pleasure several useful tables for the latitude of Upsal, and all the solar and lunar eclipses which will take place between 1712 and 1721. ... In undertaking in astronomy to facilitate the calculation of eclipses, and of the motion of the moon outside that of the syzygies, and also in undertaking to correct the tables so as to agree with the new observations, I shall have enough to do."

A letter of January, 1712, answers various questions on scientific matters referred to him by Benzelius and the Literary Society of Upsal. Among other things our young student wanted to send home some English globes, but when mounted they were very dear as well as difficult

EMANUEL SWEDENBORG

to transport, and he tried in vain to buy paper sheets to be mounted at home. Characteristically he learned to engrave on copper and drew and engraved the plates for a pair of globes. At the same time he learned from his landlord to make brass instruments, and could when at home mount the globes. Of his studies he says —

"With regard to astronomy I have made such progress in it as to have discovered much which I think will be useful in its study. Although in the beginning it made my brain ache, yet long speculations are now no longer difficult for me. I searched closely for all propositions for finding the terrestrial longitude, but could not find a single one; I have therefore originated a method by means of the moon, which is unerring, and I am certain that it is the best which has yet been advanced. In a short time I will inform the Royal Society that I have a proposition to make on this subject, stating my points. If it is favorably received by these gentlemen, I shall publish it here; if not, in France. I have also discovered many new methods for observing the planets, the moon, and the stars; that which concerns the moon and its parallaxes, diameter, and inequality,

PARENTAGE AND EARLY LIFE

I will publish whenever an opportunity arises. I am now busy working my way through algebra and the higher geometry, and I intend to make such progress in it as to be able in time to continue Polheimer's discoveries. . . . When the plates for the globes arrive in Sweden, Professor Elfvius will perhaps take care to have them printed and made up. I shall send a specimen very soon; but no impression is to be sold." In this same letter he mentions valuable English books, and names all the principal poets as well worth reading for the sake of their imagination alone. In mild terms he complains of his father's not supplying him better with money; and we find the complaint quite pardonable when we remember that the father was borrowing his children's inheritance from their mother for his own enterprises, and when we learn that Emanuel had received from him but two hundred rixdalers — about two hundred and twenty-five dollars — in sixteen months. He says it is hard to live without food or drink.

Writing again to Benzelius, August, 1712, he repeats his confidence in his new method of finding the longitude, which Dr. Halley admitted to

EMANUEL SWEDENBORG

him orally was the only good method that had been proposed. "But," he adds, "as I have not met with great encouragement here in England among this civil and proud people, I have laid it aside for some other place. When I tell them that I have some project about longitude, they treat it as an impossibility; and so I do not wish to discuss it here. . . . As my speculations made me for a time not so sociable as is serviceable and useful for me, and as my spirits are somewhat exhausted, I have taken refuge for a short time in the study of poetry, that I might be somewhat recreated by it.[1] I intend to gain a little reputation by this study on some occasion or other during this year, and I hope I may have advanced in it as much as may be expected from me; but time and others will perhaps judge of this. Still after a time I intend to take up mathematics again, although at present I am doing nothing in them; and if I am encouraged, I intend to make more discoveries in them than any one else in the present age. But without encouragement this would be sheer trouble, and it would be like *non profecturis litora*

---

[1] An early recreation of his, as shown in some verses written in his twelfth year.

PARENTAGE AND EARLY LIFE

bubus arare — ploughing the ground with stubborn steers. . . . Within three or four months, I hope with God's help to be in France; for I greatly desire to understand its fashionable and useful language. I hope by that time to have, or to find there, letters from you to some of your learned correspondents. . . . Your great kindness and your favor, of which I have had so many proofs, make me believe that your advice and your letters will induce my father to be so favorable toward me as to send me the funds which are necessary for a young man, and which will infuse into me new spirit for the prosecution of my studies. Believe me, I desire and strive to be an honor to my father's house and yours, much more strongly than you yourself can wish and endeavor. . . . I would have bought the microscope if the price had not been so much higher than I could venture to pay before receiving your orders. This microscope was one which Mr. Marshall showed to me especially; it is quite new, of his own invention, and shows the motion in fishes very vividly. There was a glass with a candle placed under it, which made the thing itself, and the object, much brighter; so that any one could see the blood in the fishes flowing swiftly, like small rivulets; for it flowed in that way, and as rapidly. At a watchmaker's I saw a curiosity which I cannot forbear mentioning. It was a clock which was still, without any motion. On the top of it was a candle, and when this was lighted, the clock began to go and to keep its true time; but as soon as the candle was blown out, the motion ceased, and so on. . . . He told me that nobody had as yet found out how it could be set in motion by the candle. Please remember me kindly to sister Anna, my dear sister Hedvig, and also to brother Ericus Benzel, the little one, about whose state of health I always desire to hear."

The next letter that has come down to us was dated Paris, August, 1713. Meanwhile Swedenborg had left London and made a considerable stay in Holland. "I left Holland," he says, "intending to make greater progress in mathematics, and also to finish all I had designed in that science. Since my arrival here I have been hindered in my work by an illness which lasted six weeks, and which interfered with my studies and other useful employments; but I have at last recovered, and am beginning to make the acquaintance of

PARENTAGE AND EARLY LIFE

the most learned men in this place. I have called upon and made the acquaintance of De La Hire, who is now a great astronomer and who was formerly a well-known geometrician. I have also been frequently with Warrignon, who is the greatest geometrician and algebraist in this city, and perhaps the greatest in Europe. About eight days ago I called upon Abbé Bignon, and presented your compliments, on the strength of which I was very favorably received by him. I submitted to him for examination, and for introduction into the Society, three discoveries, two of which were in algebra. [The third was his new method of finding longitude.] . . . Here in town I avoid conversation with Swedes, and shun all those by whom I might be in the least interrupted in my studies. What I hear from the learned, I note down at once in my journal; it would be too long to copy it out and to communicate it to you. . . . During my stay in Holland I was most of the time in Utrecht, where the Diet[1] met, and where I was in great favor with Ambassador Palmquist, who had me every day at his house; every day

[1] The famous Congress of Ambassadors, by which the Spanish Succession was ended and peace secured for a generation.

EMANUEL SWEDENBORG

also I had discussions on algebra with him. He is a good mathematician and a great algebraist. . . . In Leyden I learned glass-grinding [for telescopes], and I have now all the instruments and utensils belonging to it. . . . You may rest assured that I entertain the greatest friendship and veneration for you; I hope therefore that you will not be displeased with me on account of my silence and my delay in writing letters, if you hear that I am always intent on my studies, so that sometimes I omit more important matters."

Swedenborg's stay in Paris seems to have been less than a year, and here seems to end his aspiration for eminence in pure mathematics. For whatever reason, from this time he began to devote his attention to mechanical and practical investigations. Going from Paris by way of Hamburg to Rostock, in the north of Mecklenburg, he writes from there to Benzelius, Sept. 8, 1714 —

"I am very glad that I have come to a place where I have time and leisure to gather up all my works and thoughts, which have hitherto been without any order and are scattered here and there upon scraps of paper. I have always

PARENTAGE AND EARLY LIFE

been in want of a place and time to collect them. I have now commenced this labor and shall soon get it done. I promised my dear father to publish an academical thesis, for which I shall select some inventions in mechanics which I have at hand. Further, I have the following mechanical inventions either in hand or fully written out, namely—

" 1. The plan of a certain ship which with its men can go under the surface of the sea wherever it chooses, and do great damage to the fleet of the enemy.

" 2. A new plan for a siphon, by which a large quantity of water may be raised from any river to a higher locality in a short time.

" 3. For lifting weights by the aid of water and this portable siphon, with greater facility than by mechanical powers.

" 4. For constructing sluices in places where there is no fall of water, by means of which entire ships with their cargoes may be raised to any required height within an hour or two.

" 5. A machine driven by fire, for throwing out water; and a method of constructing it near forges where the water has no fall, but is tranquil.

EMANUEL SWEDENBORG

"6. A draw-bridge which may be closed and opened within the gates and walls.

"7. New machines for condensing and exhausting air by means of water. Also a new pump acting by water and mercury, without any siphon; which presents more advantages and works more easily than the common pumps. I have also, besides these, other new plans for pumps.

"8. A new construction of air-guns, thousands of which may be discharged in a moment by means of one siphon.

"9. A universal musical instrument, by means of which one who is quite unacquainted with music may execute all kinds of airs that are marked on paper by notes.

"10. *Sciagraphia universalis.* The universal art of delineating shades, or a mechanical method of delineating engravings of any kind upon any surface by means of fire.

"11. A water-clock in which water serves the purpose of an index, and in which by the flow of water all the moveable bodies in the heavens are demonstrated, with other curious effects.

"12. A mechanical carriage containing all

PARENTAGE AND EARLY LIFE

sorts of works which are set in motion by the movement of the horses. Also a flying carriage, or the possibility of remaining suspended in the air, and of being conveyed through it.

"13. A method of ascertaining the desires and the affections of the minds of men by analysis.

"14. New methods of constructing cords and springs, with their properties.

"These are my mechanical inventions which were heretofore lying scattered on pieces of paper, but nearly all of which are now brought into order so that when opportunity offers they may be published. To all these there is added an algebraic and a numeric calculation from which the proportions, motion, times, and all the properties which they ought to possess are deduced. Moreover, all those things which I have in analysis and astronomy require each its own place and its own time. O how I wish, my beloved friend and brother, that I could submit all these to your own eyes and to those of Professor Elfvius! But as I cannot show you the actual machines, I will at least in a short time forward you the drawings, with which I am daily occupied. I have now time also to bring my poetical efforts into order. They are only a kind of fables, like those of Ovid, under cover of which those events are treated which have happened in Europe within the last fourteen or fifteen years; so that in this manner I am allowed to sport with serious things, and to play with the heroes and the great men of our country. But meanwhile I am affected with a certain sense of shame when I reflect that I have said so much about my plans and ideas, and have not yet exhibited anything: my journey and its inconveniences have been the cause of this. I have now a great desire to return home to Sweden and to take in hand all Polheimer's inventions, make drawings, and furnish descriptions of them; and also to test them by physics, mechanics, hydrostatics, and hydraulics, and likewise by algebraic calculus. I should prefer to publish them in Sweden rather than in any other place, and in this manner to make a beginning among us of a Society for Learning and Science, for which we have such an excellent foundation in Polheimer's inventions. I wish mine could serve the same purpose. . . . A thousand remembrances to my sister Anna. I hope she is not alarmed at the approach of the Russians. I have a great longing to see little brother [nephew] Eric again; perhaps he will be able to make a triangle, or to draw one for me, when I give him a little ruler."

III

SCIENTIFIC PURSUITS AT HOME

HAVING concluded his studies abroad, Emanuel returned to the paternal home at Brunsbo in 1715. Then his father, in accordance with the custom of the times, made application to Government to give him employment. Meanwhile Emanuel makes preparation for the scientific periodical he had projected and seeks to bring into service some of his inventions, of which he writes to Benzelius—

"I looked very carefully for the machines which I some time ago sent to my father; they were eight in number, but I was unable to discover the place in which he had laid them aside. He thinks they have been sent to you, which I hope with all my heart; for it cost me a great amount of work to put them on paper, and I shall not have any time during the next winter to do this over again. There were, First, three drawings and plans for water-pumps, by which a large quantity of water can be raised in a short time

SCIENTIFIC PURSUITS AT HOME

from any sea or lake you choose. Second, two machines for raising weights by means of water, as easily and quickly as is done by mechanical forces. Third, some kinds of sluices, which can be constructed where there is no fall of water, and which will raise boats over hills, sand-banks, etc. Fourth, a machine to discharge by air ten or eleven thousand shots per hour. All these machines are carefully described and calculated algebraically. I had further intended to communicate plans of some kinds of vessels and boats, in which persons may go under water whenever they choose; also a machine for building at pleasure a blast furnace near any still water, where the wheel will nevertheless revolve by means of the fire, which will put the water in motion; likewise some kinds of air-guns that are loaded in a moment, and discharge sixty or seventy shots in succession without any fresh charge. Toward winter perhaps I shall draw and describe these machines. I should like to have the opportunity and the means of setting one or other of them up and getting it to work.

"The day after to-morrow I will travel to the Kinnekulle, to select a spot for a small observa-

III

SCIENTIFIC PURSUITS AT HOME

HAVING concluded his studies abroad, Emanuel returned to the paternal home at Brunsbo in 1715. Then his father, in accordance with the custom of the times, made application to Government to give him employment. Meanwhile Emanuel makes preparation for the scientific periodical he had projected and seeks to bring into service some of his inventions, of which he writes to Benzelius—

"I looked very carefully for the machines which I some time ago sent to my father; they were eight in number, but I was unable to discover the place in which he had laid them aside. He thinks they have been sent to you, which I hope with all my heart; for it cost me a great amount of work to put them on paper, and I shall not have any time during the next winter to do this over again. There were, First, three drawings and plans for water-pumps, by which a large quantity of water can be raised in a short time

SCIENTIFIC PURSUITS AT HOME

from any sea or lake you choose. Second, two machines for raising weights by means of water, as easily and quickly as is done by mechanical forces. Third, some kinds of sluices, which can be constructed where there is no fall of water, and which will raise boats over hills, sand-banks, etc. Fourth, a machine to discharge by air ten or eleven thousand shots per hour. All these machines are carefully described and calculated algebraically. I had further intended to communicate plans of some kinds of vessels and boats, in which persons may go under water whenever they choose; also a machine for building at pleasure a blast furnace near any still water, where the wheel will nevertheless revolve by means of the fire, which will put the water in motion; likewise some kinds of air-guns that are loaded in a moment, and discharge sixty or seventy shots in succession without any fresh charge. Toward winter perhaps I shall draw and describe these machines. I should like to have the opportunity and the means of setting one or other of them up and getting it to work.

"The day after to-morrow I will travel to the Kinnekulle, to select a spot for a small observatory, where I intend toward winter to make some observations respecting our horizon, and to lay a foundation for those observations by which my invention on the longitude of places may be confirmed. Perhaps I may then travel in all haste first to Upsal, to get some things I need for it."

At this time, having recently returned from France, in one letter to Benzelius he says, "Pardon, my dear brother, that I write to you in French. But the language in which you think usually suits you best. My thoughts at present move in this language; but whenever Cicero shall again engage me, I shall endeavor to address you like a Ciceronian." He was now much in conference with the eminent Swedish engineer Polheimer — soon to be ennobled by Charles XII and given the name Polhem — and he urged the founding of a department of Mechanics in the university, in which both Polheimer and he himself would have appointments. But his labors were bestowed chiefly on his scientific periodical, called *Dædalus*, in which his own and Polheimer's inventions and discoveries were set forth in detail. On the 26th of June, 1716, he writes to his brother Benzelius —

SCIENTIFIC PURSUITS AT HOME

" I am engaged on the subject which I intend for the last number of this year, and which I shall finish this week, namely, Polheimer's ideas upon the resistance of mediums, which at first were written down in Latin, and which have cost me a great deal of labor and mental exertion to reduce into such a form as will please the Assessor and the learned; likewise my method of finding the longitude of places, which I warrant to be certain and sure. I must hear what the learned say about it."

On the 4th of September he writes again to the same —

"I am very glad that *Dædalus*, part iii, has appeared. I thank you for having taken so much trouble and care with it: when I am present with you, I will thank you still more. I am already thinking of the contents of part v of the *Dædalus*. I think it will be best for me, first, to put down Assessor Polheimer's ingenious tap, with a sufficient mechanic and algebraic description; second, to make an addition to the description of his 'Blankstötz' machine, as this is a work which requires greater accuracy, reflection, and consideration than it has yet received; third, to leave room for some of the eclipses observed by Professor Elfvius, by which the longitude of Upsal is also obtained. If you would honor our little work with a life of Stiernhjelm, or with something else from the history of the learned, I know that thereby our publication would become more interesting; as in this case the heavy matter would be relieved by more pleasing subjects. I know also that this would gain us the favor and approbation of many, as the literary world acknowledges you as by far its best member; I hope therefore that this honor will not be refused. May God grant you a long life, although I am afraid that your many studies will deprive us of this benefit, by shortening your days: for I know no one who has more consideration for his various studies, and less for himself. All the learned and the Muses entreat you to spare yourself, and in you the Muses. It is worthy of all praise indeed to offer up one's self to the Muses, but not on the very altar; it is easy enough to become a premature victim. Pardon this admonition, my brother; your letter to my father is the cause of it. I hope that my little learning and my *Dædalus* will be long under your auspices. I think of

SCIENTIFIC PURSUITS AT HOME

inserting in the fourth number some Dædalian speculations about a flying machine, and to leave room for Dr. Bromell's curiosities, if he be pleased to insert them. Assessor Polheimer writes that in the following number he wishes to insert such matter as will be of use to the public — such as water and wind machines, mill, etc. — of which I am very glad."

Charles XII had now returned to Sweden, to the great joy of his people, and found much use for both Polheimer and Swedenborg. In December, 1716, Swedenborg writes to Benzelius —

"I wrote you a letter from Lund and should have written to you more frequently had I not been prevented by my mechanical and other occupations; moreover I had enough to attend to in order to accomplish my design. Since his Majesty graciously looked at my *Dædalus* and its plan, he has advanced me to the post of an Assessor Extraordinary in the College of Mines, yet in such a way that I should for some time attend the Councillor of Commerce, Polheimer. What pleases me most is that his Majesty pronounced so favorable and gracious a judgment respecting me, and himself defended me against

EMANUEL SWEDENBORG

those who thought the worst of me; and that he has since promised me his further favor and protection, of which I have been assured both directly and indirectly. But let me tell you all more in detail. After his Majesty had sufficiently inquired as to my character, studies, and the like, and I being so fortunate as to have good references, he offered me three posts and offices to choose from, and afterward gave me the warrant for the rank and post of an Assessor Extraordinary. But as my enemies played too many intrigues with the above-mentioned warrant and couched it in ambiguous terms, I sent it back to his Majesty with some comments, well knowing whom I had to depend upon; when there was immediately granted me a new one, and likewise a gracious letter to the College of Mines. My opponent had to sit down at the King's own table and write this out in duplicate in two forms, of which the King selected the best; so that those who had sought to injure me were glad to escape with honor and reputation, they had so nearly burned their fingers.

"*Dædalus* has enjoyed the favor of lying these three weeks upon his Majesty's table, and has

SCIENTIFIC PURSUITS AT HOME

furnished matter for many discussions and questions; it has also been shown by his Majesty to many persons. Within a short time I intend to send you what is to follow for *Dædalus*, part v; when perhaps Drs. Roberg and Bromell will not refuse to honor it with their contributions; they might possibly derive some profit from it.

"We arrived here at Carlscrona a few days ago, intending after three weeks to go to Gottenburg, and afterward to Trollhätta, Lakes Wener and Hjelmar, and Gullspångelf, in order to examine sites for sluices and locks, a plan which meets with his Majesty's entire approbation. ... A thousand kind remembrances to sister Anna. The kid gloves have been purchased."

From these letters of what we may still call Swedenborg's youth, we learn better than from any description its exuberance, its energy, its assurance of mathematical power, its fertility of invention, and its strong desire to be employed in practical works for the good of mankind. Mingled with these traits it is pleasant to see the warm, confiding love that overflows to the brother and sister who had cared for and directed his budding manhood, and were still to him as father and mother. The traits are the natural ones of the time of life. What we specially observe with Swedenborg is their vigor and power, eminent by inheritance, and conserved in remarkable degree by a freedom from all ignoble passions and weak indulgence, which we can attribute only to the protection that came with a deep sense of duty to God and to man. His appointment as Assessor in the College of Mines now gave him at twenty-eight years of age his eagerly sought opportunity for practical service to his country, happily in the line of his scientific and mechanical studies. This was the form of the appointment:—

"CHARLES, by the grace of God, King of Sweden, Gothia, and Wendia, etc. Our especial favor and gracious pleasure, under God Almighty, to the true men and servants, to our Council and President, as well as Vice-President, and to all the Members of the College of Mines. Inasmuch as we have graciously deigned to command that Emanuel Swedberg shall be Assessor Extraordinary in the College of Mines, although he at the same time is to attend Polheimer, the Councillor

SCIENTIFIC PURSUITS AT HOME

of Commerce, and to be of assistance to him in his engineering works, and in carrying out his designs, — therefore it is our pleasure hereby to let you know this, with our gracious command, and that you allow him a seat and voice in the College whenever he be present, and especially whenever any business be brought forward pertaining to mechanics. We hereby commend you, especially and graciously, to God Almighty.

"CAROLUS.

"LUND, December 18, 1716."

The College of Mines consisted of a President, always of the highest order of nobility, two councillors of mines, and some six assessors. Under its charge the whole mining interest of Sweden was placed. From its records it appears that on April 6, 1717, Mr. Emanuel Swedberg, appointed by his Majesty to be Assessor Extraordinary in the College of Mines, being present, "As a beginning of his introduction, the royal decree which had been received was read. Afterward the above-named Assessor, after delivering to the Royal College the formulary of the oath signed by himself, took the oath of loyalty and of office, with

EMANUEL SWEDENBORG

his hand upon the Book, and then took the seat belonging to him."

With this simple, solemn induction into his office, Swedenborg entered upon his labors to which he gave strict attention, unremitted save on leave of his sovereign in the pursuit of his studies, for thirty years; with what satisfaction to the College and to the Government we shall learn when we find him asking permission to retire. The office was a favorable one, demanding his best talent and energy, yet not so engrossing as to prevent his pursuing private studies. Except in the summer months, when the members of the College usually visited the mines, daily meetings were held in Stockholm, at which Swedenborg was punctual in attendance, when not in service elsewhere. For a while, however, by the command of Charles he was kept away in assisting Polhem — as Polheimer was called on being ennobled. Nor by the King's wish did he fail to continue his *Dædalus*. On the 23d of February, 1717, he writes to Benzelius —

"Enclosed I send *Dædalus*, part v, and I most humbly solicit you to extend to it the kindness that you have shown toward the former

SCIENTIFIC PURSUITS AT HOME

numbers. I should have finished it long ago, but I have been continually on a journey of ever changing direction, which scarce left me an hour's time for such work. But as I have now arrived at Stiernsund, I have found an opportunity for a few days to get this up as well as I can. I hope it will win the approval of the Upsal people, and especially your own.

"I have added the Latin to it on the opposite page, according to his Majesty's wish, who pointed out to me where the Swedish should be and where the Latin. . . .

"As his Majesty seemed to be interested in the manufacture of salt in Sweden, we gathered minute information about it in Uddevalla; and we found that in Sweden there are the best opportunities for its manufacture, as there is abundance of forest and water for promoting the work. . . . Should such a work be established, it would profit the country more than the whole of its iron manufacture, in which a loss is occasionally sustained; but in the case of salt there would be a real gain and the money would remain in the country.

"We hope that our journey hither will in time

be of importance. At Trollhätta, Gullspångelf, and Lake Hjelmar also, we found everything feasible, and at less expense than had been anticipated. If I do nothing more in the matter, I act at least as a stimulus in it.

"Will you please remember me kindly to little brother Eric. I hear that his love for mechanics and drawing continues. If he can give the slip to his preceptor, I should like to induce him to follow me; when I would try in every way to promote his welfare, to instruct him in mathematics and other things, should it be desired. Please remember me also a hundred times to sister Anna."

The project referred to in this and a preceding letter, for which Swedenborg and Polhem had visited Trollhätta, was to connect the North and the Baltic seas by a canal, thus saving the long détour about the southern peninsula and the exposure to the hostile Danes, at Elsinore. It was a project of Bishop Brask in 1526, discovered by Benzelius and communicated by Swedenborg to Charles XII, who embraced it eagerly, but was prevented by death from completing it. As completed in more recent times the canal follows in great part the course undertaken by Polhem and

SCIENTIFIC PURSUITS AT HOME

Swedenborg, and a disused portion still bears the name of Swedenborg.

In January, 1718, Swedenborg writes to Benzelius declining his offer to seek for him the then vacated professorship of Astronomy at Upsal, for the reason that he had now full employment in more practical matters and in the study of mechanics. He concludes, "I have five little treatises which I desire to lay before my friends; one, which I have finished to-day, is on the round particles, in which Dr. Roberg will probably be interested, for he is well skilled in all that concerns these least things, and is delighted with such subjects."

In these extracts from Swedenborg's letters, of which we have more at this period of his life than at any other, we copy without reserve whatever seems to throw any light on his character and on the nature of his pursuits. The entire collection is to be found in Tafel's Documents, in which it makes one hundred and seventy octavo pages. During the publication of the *Dædalus*, from 1716 to 1718, Swedenborg published little else. A small tract in Swedish on the tinware of Stiernsund, 1717, is attributed to him; and it is probable that

EMANUEL SWEDENBORG

his Algebra, a 16mo of 135 pages, was printed in 1718. Of works of this period in manuscript there are still preserved an essay on the Importance of Instituting an Astronomical Observatory in Sweden; one on the Causes of Things; a New Theory concerning the End of the Earth, in which he holds that the earth revolves in a resisting medium and is gradually retarding its motion and approaching the sun; a Project for Assisting Commerce and Manufactures, by controlling the export of Swedish iron and copper; a Memorial on the Establishment of Salt-works in Sweden; an Essay on the Nature of Fire and Colors; and some discussions of higher mathematics, involving the Differential and Integral Calculus. Of the direction of his studies at this time, the following letter to Benzelius, written 30th January, 1718, gives further information: —

"I send you something new in physics, on the particles of air and water, proving them to be round, which may militate against the philosophy of many; but as I base my theory upon experience and geometry, I do not expect that any one can refute it by arguments. Preconceived ideas received from Descartes and others will be the

SCIENTIFIC PURSUITS AT HOME

greatest obstacle to it, and will cause objections. Dr. Roberg, who in everything that is minute and subtile is himself subtile, is best able to judge respecting it: if you would therefore be kind enough to leave this with him, I should like to hear his opinion. If Professor Valerius would lay aside his own and his father's Cartesianism, his opinion would also be valuable to me. I have materials enough on this subject to fill a large book, as is done by the learned with their speculations abroad; but as we have no appliances here for such large publications, I must cut my coat according to the cloth and introduce only the most general views. The use of this seems to me to enable us to investigate more thoroughly the nature of air and water in all its parts: for if the true shape of the particles is once discovered, we obtain with it all the properties which belong to such a shape. I hope that this rests on a solid foundation. In future I should not wish to publish anything which has not better ground to rest upon than the former things in the *Dædalus*."

In the summer of the same year by the King's command he was engaged in the construction of the above-mentioned Baltic and North Sea canal. In September he writes to his brother-in-law —

"I found his Majesty most gracious toward me, much more so than I had any reason to expect, which I regard as a good omen. Count Mörner also showed me all the favor that I could wish.

"Every day I had some mathematical matters for his Majesty, who deigned to be pleased with all of them. When the eclipse took place, I took his Majesty out to see it, and talked much to him about it. This, however, is a mere beginning. I hope in time to be able to do something in this quarter for the advancement of science, but I do not wish to bring anything forward now except what is of immediate use. His majesty found considerable fault with me for not having continued my *Dædalus*; but I pleaded want of means, of which he does not like to hear. I expect some assistance for it very soon.

"With respect to brother Esberg [a nephew of Benzelius], I will see that he gets some employment at the locks; but nothing can be done before next spring. If he meanwhile studies mathematics well and begins to make models, it

SCIENTIFIC PURSUITS AT HOME

will be perhaps of use to him. I wish very much that little brother Ericus was grown up. I believe that next spring, if everything remain as it is, I shall begin the building of a lock myself and shall have my own command; in which case I hope to be of service to one or the other. I receive only three dalers a day at present at the canal works, but I hope soon to receive more.

"Polhem's eldest daughter is betrothed to a chamberlain of the King, of the name of Manderström. I wonder what people will say about this, inasmuch as she was engaged [by her father] to me. His second daughter is in my opinion much prettier.

"How is Professor Valerius? I should be very glad to hear of his health and good condition. Remember me to sister Anna."

Polhem's second daughter, Emerentia, was young at this time, not quite sixteen, and did not, it would appear, reciprocate Swedenborg's tender feeling. Her father, it is said, gave him a written claim upon her in the future, in the hope that she would become more yielding, and this contract she was obliged to sign. But she fretted about it so much every day that her brother was moved with compassion and purloined the contract from Swedenborg, whose only comfort consisted in daily perusing it, and who therefore quickly missed his treasure. His sorrow at his loss was so evident that her father insisted on knowing the cause; and on learning it, was willing by an exercise of his authority to have the lost document restored. But when Swedenborg himself saw her grief, he voluntarily relinquished his right and left the house with, it is said, a solemn vow never to fix his affections on any woman again. However this may have been, it is certain that he never married and that he never forgot his first love. What called Swedenborg to Strömstadt he does not explain. But from other sources we learn that he was engaged in superintending the transportation of two galleys, five large boats, and a sloop seventeen miles overland, from Strömstadt to Iderfjol, for the aid of Charles XII in his operations against Frederickshall. Baron Sandels in his eulogy gives the credit of the feat to Swedenborg, and in fact we have seen that several years before he had drawn out plans for such transportation; but we do not know whether the plan adopted was his or Polhem's.

SCIENTIFIC PURSUITS AT HOME

In October of the same year, 1718, he writes again from his father's home at Brunsbo —

"*Most honored and dear brother*, — I am just starting for Carlsgraf, after having been here about three weeks. Meanwhile I have seen *Dædalus*, part vi, through the press. It contains the following articles: 1. Directions for Pointing Mortars, by C. Polhem; 2. An Easy Way of Counting Balls which are Stored in the Shape of a Triangle, by Em. S——; 3. Useful Directions in Ship-Building; 4. A Proof that our Vital Nature consists of Small Tremulations, with a great Number of Experiments; 5. Respecting a Curve the Secant of which forms Right Angles with it. I have sent this, the figures and letter-press, to his Majesty. As soon as I have an opportunity I will send it over to you."

The close of this year, 1718, was the close of the life of Charles XII, killed on his expedition to Norway, and the end of his important projects. It is a year later when we hear again from Swedenborg, writing from Stockholm to Benzelius —

"What I have in hand consists, first, of a minute description of our Swedish blast-furnaces;

secondly, of a theory or an investigation into the nature of fire and stoves, in which I have collected everything I could gather from blacksmiths, charcoal-burners, roasters of ore, superintendents of iron-furnaces, etc.; and upon this the theory is based. I hope that the many discoveries which I have made therein will in time prove useful. For instance, a fire may be made in some new stoves for warming, where the wood and coal which usually last a day will last six days, and will give out more heat. Vice-President Hjärne has approved of this in all its particulars, and if desired I can show the proof of it. The former of these treatises I handed in to-day to the Royal College of Mines.

"I have also written a little anatomy of our vital forces, which, I maintain, consist of tremulations. For this purpose I made myself thoroughly acquainted with the anatomy of the nerves and membranes; and I have proved the harmony which exists between that and the interesting geometry of tremulations — together with many other ideas in which I found that I agreed with those of Baglivius. The day before yesterday I handed them in to the Royal Medical College.

SCIENTIFIC PURSUITS AT HOME

"Besides this, I have improved the little treatise which was published at Upsal about the high water in primeval times; and I have added a number of clear proofs, together with an undeniable demonstration how stones were moved in a deep ocean. I have also adduced arguments to show how the northern horizon was changed, and that it is reasonable to suppose that Sweden in the primeval ages was an island. This I have handed in to the Censor of Books, so as to publish it anew. There is also quite a number of smaller papers. The deep study by which I have endeavored to compass these subjects has caused me to look with contempt upon everything I have heretofore published; but I intend to improve them very much when they are to be translated [from Swedish into French or Latin]. . . .

"With much love, I remain your most faithful servant, EMAN. SWEDENBORG."

This is the first letter we have in which Swedenborg assumes the new name which had been given in June to the wife and children of Bishop Swedberg, with admission to the equestrian order of the nobility, and so to a seat in the Diet —

EMANUEL SWEDENBORG

an honor granted by the new Queen, Ulrica Eleonora, younger sister of Charles XII, out of the friendly regard she had always shown for the independent clergyman, and in return perhaps for his support of the royal power.

The essays here referred to are still preserved, but most of their subjects were afterward treated at much greater length. In the till then little explored field of geology Swedenborg's study of the mines of Sweden gave him eagerly grasped opportunity, and as in everything else, though not making it a specialty, he carried his observations and conclusions far ahead of his time. Prof. Alfred G. Nathorst in his "Geology of Sweden," 1892, credits Swedenborg with being the first to conclude from various observations that Sweden was formerly covered with the sea, a large part of its rocks having been formed of marine deposits. He says —

"As a whole it may be regarded as distinctive of Swedenborg's method of demonstration that where possible he seeks to confirm the correctness of his position by means of experiment. He may therefore be regarded as one of the first in the field of experimental geology. . . . [Quite

SCIENTIFIC PURSUITS AT HOME

in accordance with most modern conclusion] he denies that the whole interior of the earth is in a glowing state, and thinks that the volcanoes receive their nourishment from melted masses in the earth's crust."[1]

Three weeks later, Swedenborg writes again to Benzelius, "I am delighted to hear that what I wrote you in my last was to your liking." He adds some further argument to show that no sudden approach to the sun is taking place. Incidentally he brings in his theory of the vortical energy which controls the solar system, and also each world in itself, but in too brief terms to be cited as a statement of the theory. At greater length he gives reasons for thinking that the sun cannot be, as some had conjectured, the abode of the damned. He would rather suspect that there is the abode of the blessed; since from the sun is all the heat, light, and life of the world, indeed the most refined elements of existence, where we might look for that which is above and within matter, and might even imagine the seat of God Himself.

[1] Letter of Alfred H. Stroh, May 31, 1903, in *The New Philosophy.*

EMANUEL SWEDENBORG

Here we have a ready basis for Swedenborg's later understanding that God is in the Sun of heaven, and that through this Sun He sends life and force into the sun of this world, for the support of material existence. As to the fires of the damned, he suggests that the pain of burning is the effect of destruction of tissue, which cannot be what is meant in the Bible; but rather he thinks the remorses of conscience might be a sufficiently strong fire. In this, too, he is approaching the doctrine he afterward taught, that the fires of hell are the fires of selfish passion. But he piously concludes, "I hope that my philosophizing may not be misinterpreted; for, after all, the foundation is God's Word."

On the 1st of December he writes again —

"*Most honored and dearest brother,* — I send you herewith the little work which I mentioned in my last respecting a decimal system in our coinage and measures. This is the last that I will publish myself, because every-day and home affairs grow of small account, and because I have already worked myself poor by them. I have been singing long enough; let us see whether any one

SCIENTIFIC PURSUITS AT HOME

will come forward and hand me some bread in return.

"There are, however, some plans which I have entertained for some time, and which at last have assumed a definite shape. I should like to see how far they meet with your approval: First, to translate what I have published into Latin or French, and to send it then to Holland and England; to which I should like to add, by way of improvement, some of my discoveries about fire and stones, and about some improvements in mining matters; besides some other papers which are not yet printed. Would you be kind enough to give the names of some who write scientific papers and memoirs? Second, as I think I now in some measure understand the mechanics which are of use in mining districts and in mines, so far at least as to be able better than any one else to describe what is new and old there, and further to understand the theory of fire and stones, as to which I have made quite a number of discoveries, I intend to spend all my remaining time upon what may promote everything that concerns mining, and on the basis which has already been laid, in collecting as much information as possible. Third,

EMANUEL SWEDENBORG

if fortune so favors me that I shall be provided with all the means that are required, and if meanwhile by the above preparations and communications I shall have gained some credit abroad, I should prefer by all means to go abroad and seek my fortune in my calling, which consists in promoting everything that concerns the administration and working of mines. For he is nothing short of a fool who is independent and at liberty to do as he pleases and sees an opportunity for himself abroad and yet remains at home in darkness and cold, where the Furies, Envy, and Pluto have taken up their abode and dispose the rewards, and where labors such as I have performed are rewarded with misery. The only thing I would desire until that time comes is *bene latere*, to find a sequestered place where I can live secluded from the world. I think I may find such a corner in the end either at Starbo or at Skinskatteberg. But as this would take four or five years' time, I am quite ready to acknowledge that long-laid plans are like long roofs, apt to tumble in; for man proposes, God disposes. Still I have always been in favor of a man's knowing what he is doing, and of his forming for himself some clever plan

SCIENTIFIC PURSUITS AT HOME

of what it is most practicable for him to carry out in his life. I remain, most honored and dear brother,

"Your most faithful servant and brother,
"EMAN. SWEDENBORG."

The last letter to Benzelius preserved for us containing much information about his studies, is dated May 2, 1720 —

"I am at present engaged in examining all the chemistry contained in the treasury of the Sudeman Library, which belongs now to Hesselius; for I have proposed to myself to examine thoroughly everything that concerns fire and metals, *a primis incunabulis usque ad maturitatem*, according to the plan of the memorandum which has been already communicated to you. I take the chemical experiments of Boyle, Reucher, Hjärne, Simons, and others, and trace out nature in its least things, instituting comparisons with geometry and mechanics. I am also encouraged every day by new discoveries as to the nature of these subtile substances; and as I am beginning to see that experience in an uninterrupted series seems to be inclined to agree therewith, I am becoming more and more confirmed in my ideas. It seems to me that the immense number of experiments that have been made affords a good ground for building upon; and that the toil and expenses incurred by others may be turned to use by working up with head what they have collected with their hands. Many deductions may thus be made which will be of use in chemistry and metallurgy, and in determining the nature of fire and other things."

IV

FURTHER STUDIES AND PUBLICATIONS ABROAD

As Assessor Extraordinary Swedenborg received no salary except when in actual service, of which little was required after the death of Charles XII; and accordingly in June, 1720, he presented a petition to the Royal College of Mines stating that he had spent all his time and money in perfecting himself in what would be of service to his country, and therefore begging the College graciously to provide him with some salary or other support by virtue of his appointment. A year later he wrote to the President and College —

" As I am about to undertake a new journey abroad, it is my duty to make it known to your Excellency and to the Honorable College in writing; especially as my only object is to collect more minute information respecting the condition of the mines abroad and the processes which are followed there, and also to make inquiries respecting commerce, so far as it relates to metals."

EMANUEL SWEDENBORG

Of this visit abroad we have the following summary from his Itinerary : —

"In the spring of 1721 I again went abroad, going to Holland by Copenhagen and Hamburg. There I published my *Prodromus Principiorum Rerum Naturalium,* and several other short treatises in octavo. From Holland I travelled to Aix-la-Chapelle, Liege, Cologne, and other adjacent places, examining the mines there. Thence I went to Leipsic, where I published my *Miscellanea Observata.* Leaving that town I visited all the mines in Saxony, and then returned to Hamburg. From Hamburg I returned to Brunswick and Goslar, and visited all the mines in the Hartz Mountains belonging to the houses of Hanover and Lüneburg. The father-in-law of a son of the Emperor and of a son of the Czar, Duke Louis Rudolph, who resided at Blankenburg, graciously defrayed all my expenses; and on taking leave of him he presented me with a gold medal and a large silver coffee-pot, besides bestowing upon me many other marks of his favor. I then returned to Hamburg, and thence, by way of Stralsund and Ystad, to Stockholm, having been absent one year and three months."

STUDIES AND PUBLICATIONS ABROAD

The two Latin treatises, the publication of which is here briefly mentioned, have been translated and published in London under the respective titles of "Some Specimens of a Work on the Principles of Chemistry," and "Miscellaneous Observations connected with the Physical Sciences." In the first-named volume are included also three other publications of Swedenborg, of the same year, **New O**bservations and Discoveries respecting Iron and Fire; A **N**ew Method of Finding the Longitudes of Places; and A **N**ew Method of Constructing Docks and Dykes. These essays give a fair specimen of Swedenborg's manner of treating scientific subjects. He first collects the observations and experiments of others, adding a few of his own, and then, with geometry for a guide, searches for the hidden causes and operations of nature. His theory of matter, as well summarized by one of his ablest translators, Dr. J. J. Garth Wilkinson, is "that roundness is the form adapted to motion; that the particles of fluids, and specifically of water, are round, hollow spherules, with a subtile matter, identical with ether or caloric, in their interiors and interstices; that the crust, or crustal portion, of each particle is itself formed of lesser particles, and these again of lesser, and so forth — water being in this way the sixth dimension, or the result of the sixth grouping of the particles; that the interstices of the fluids furnish the original moulds of the solids, and the rows of crustal particles forced off one by one by various agencies, furnish the matter of the same; that after solid particles are thus cast in their appropriate moulds, their fracture, aggregation, the filling-in of their pores and interstices by lesser particles, and a number of other and accidental conditions, provide the units of the multiform substances of which the mineral kingdom is composed. According to this theory, then, there is but one substance in the world, namely, the first; the difference of things is difference of form; there are no positive, but only relative, atoms; no metaphysical, but only real elements; moreover, the heights of chemical doctrine can be scaled by rational induction alone, planted on the basis of analysis, synthesis, and observation."

To the above may be added that Swedenborg's crustal particles bear to the interior and interstitial space the ratio in volume of one to two, and

STUDIES AND PUBLICATIONS ABROAD

in weight that of eight to one — a coincidence with the ratios of the later discovered elements that is highly suggestive. Dumas, in his Chemical Philosophy, remarks of Swedenborg, "It is then to him we are indebted for the first idea of making cubes, tetraedrons, pyramids, and the different crystalline forms, by grouping the spheres."

At the same time with these deep investigations he was also engaged with all earnestness in promoting the working of mines and metals, and on his return home he attempted to introduce an entirely new method of reducing copper ore, as described in his treatise on Copper published twelve years later. In the spring of 1723, though not yet an Ordinary Assessor, he became a regular attendant at the sittings of the College, except when abroad or engaged in the sessions of the Diet, of which by the ennoblement of the family he now became member. In place of speeches at the Diet, none of which have been preserved, we have memorials presented by him not without interest at the present day. The following was perhaps his first address, read to the Diet, February 7, 1723: —

"The chief cause of a country's increase in

wealth is the balance of commerce: if its imports are greater than a country can pay with its own products, it follows that it loses annually considerable sums by leaving them in the hands of foreign nations; besides, it diminishes the capital which it collected under more favorable circumstances, and which it should hand down to posterity. As soon also as a country by an imprudent course suddenly falls into poverty, it unavoidably sinks in the estimation of other nations, and they refuse any longer to trade with it, although in former times they may have enriched themselves by its wealth and sucked out its substance and marrow. Yea, more serious consequences still may ensue; for unless a watchful eye is kept on the balance of a country's trade, a general want may be caused thereby which makes itself felt in the private circumstances of every one; fortunes and possessions in the land are diminished in value; no means are forthcoming for the support of the navy and army; the defence of the country becomes weak and impotent; the public servants must be satisfied with small salaries; manufactures and agriculture together with all the moneys invested in them depreciate in value; besides other

STUDIES AND PUBLICATIONS ABROAD

contingencies which in such a case overtake the higher as well as the lower ranks, and especially the business men, who must suffer most heavily from it."

He then presents two computations: the first showing the average imports and exports during the reign of Charles XI, when Swedish commerce was most flourishing; and the second showing the balance of trade at the time of the memorial. In the first case the balance of exports was four and a half million florins in favor of Sweden, and in the second case the balance was from two and a half to three millions against the country. "From which," he says, "it follows that the rich products of Sweden are no longer sufficient to pay the excess of imported goods and merchandise, but that annually a part of the cash property of the country has to be employed to adjust the difference. . . . As every one now is left in freedom to express his well-meant thoughts, and to suggest how the common weal is likely to be best helped, it is hoped that it will not be unfavorably received if I insist, in all humility, that there is nothing the present Diet can do of greater importance than to examine and to assist and promote all propositions which have for their purpose to infuse new life into Swedish commerce, so as to make our balance even; and this for the sake of the private welfare of every one of us and also for that of our whole posterity." Next he shows that Sweden has lost, first, the revenues formerly derived from various provinces that have been conquered by Russia and Denmark; second, the freighting business which she formerly enjoyed, but which during her wars and by the decay of her shipping has gone into foreign hands; third, her former profitable commerce with the now lost provinces. Finally, he points out Swedish iron and copper mining interests as the most important in the balance of trade, and most worthy of attention, and concludes with recommending careful inquiry how the mercantile marine may be built up, unnecessary importation checked or cheapened, and domestic manufactures developed and protected.

On the 18th of the same month Swedenborg memorializes the Diet against the rule and law of the country which requires the mining of a baser metal to give way to that of a more noble, even when, as he shows, the mining of the baser by

STUDIES AND PUBLICATIONS ABROAD

its greater abundance may be many-fold more valuable.

In the following May he had occasion to present another and longer memorial to the same purport, in consequence of instructions given by the Diet to the Royal College of Mines to pay special attention to the mining of silver and copper. He showed that the yearly production of iron in Sweden was equivalent to fifty tons of gold, and that of copper was equivalent to less than fifteen tons. While then he would have the copper mines cherished and protected, he would not have it done at the expense of the iron mines. Yet he seems to have been opposed in these common-sense views by his own colleagues of the Royal College of Mines, on what ground we do not know.

About the same time he presented another memorial to the Diet, setting forth the fact that Swedish iron was then exported in pigs to Holland, whence it was re-shipped inland to Liege and Sauerland, where it was puddled and rolled into bar or sheet iron, then carried back to Holland and exported at great profit to various countries. This profit, he declares, with small expense and industry might be kept at home. He accompanies his memorial with drawings and details of the puddling furnaces and rolling-mills abroad, and simply submits the expediency of encouragement by the Government to those who will undertake the manufacture in Sweden.

The treatment which this eminently reasonable and practical memorial received at the hands of the Diet and the Royal College of Mines goes far to convince us that Swedenborg had reason to complain of the want of response to his genius in his own country and home. The memorial was read before the Committee on the business of the Diet, April 20, 1723; by them it was referred to the Committee on Mining and Commerce, where it was read May 7th. By the Diet it was referred to the King, by whom it was submitted to the Royal College of Mines and to that of Commerce, Aug. 10, 1725. It arrived in the Royal College of Mines, Aug. 23, 1725, and was filed for future reference, Sept. 1, 1726. In the course of three years and a half, a matter which would properly have commended itself for instant action is filed away for future reference! So slow were the Swedes to manufacture the Swedes iron, now in demand throughout the world.

STUDIES AND PUBLICATIONS ABROAD

On the 15th of July, 1724, a Royal warrant was issued by King Frederick appointing the wellborn Assessor Emanuel Swedenborg a regular Assessor in the Royal College, with a salary of eight hundred dalers [1] in silver. This was not the full salary of the office, which was twelve hundred dalers, but was increased to it six years later. Of the following ten years employed in public duties we have no details, but know from his later publications that together with his official duties Swedenborg was diligently pursuing the course of study he had adopted. Early in the year 1733 he asked from the King leave of absence for nine months, in which to go to Germany and see through the press his great work entitled as a whole, *Opera Philosophica et Mineralia*. Of this there were three noble folio volumes, printed at the expense of his friend the Duke of Brunswick. The first volume had the special title of *Principia Rerum Naturalium*, or First Principles of Natural Things; the other two treated of the working of iron and copper. Of the *Principia* its English translator, the Reverend Augustus Clissold, says —

[1] About $450.

EMANUEL SWEDENBORG

"The First Part treats of the origin and laws of motion, and is mostly devoted to the consideration of its first principles; which are investigated philosophically, then geometrically, their existence being traced from a first natural point down to the formation of a solar vortex, and afterwards from the solar vortex to the successive constitution of the elements and of the three kingdoms of nature. From the first element to the last compound, it is the author's object to show that effort or conatus to motion tends to a spiral figure; and that there is an actual motion of particles constituting a solar chaos, which is spiral and consequently vortical.

"In the Second Part the author applies this theory of vortical motion to the phenomena of magnetism, by which on the one hand he endeavors to test the truth of his principles, and on the other by application of the principles to explain the phenomena of magnetism; the motion of the magnetical effluvia being as in the former case considered to be vortical.

"In the Third Part the author applies the same principles of motion to Cosmogony, including the origination of the planetary bodies from the sun,

STUDIES AND PUBLICATIONS ABROAD

and their vortical revolutions until they arrived at their present orbit; likewise to the constitution and laws of the different elements, the motions of all which are alleged to be vortical; likewise to the constitution and laws of the three kingdoms of nature, the animal, vegetable, and mineral: so that the entire *Principia* aims to establish a true theory of the vortices, founded upon a true system of corpuscular philosophy."

The *Principia* is too deeply mathematical and reasoned with too subtile intuition for common readers to follow. For this reason, in part, it has been neglected by later scientists; but also because they with more perfect instruments have devoted their attention chiefly to experimental observation. For a century the atomic theory sufficed them, but now they are going far deeper and are closely approximating Swedenborg's theory of matter as compounded of first finites — as he calls them — in intense vortical motion. Not that this theory was originated by him. It was held in a way by the old Greek philosopher, Anaxagoras, and was revived by Descartes. But Swedenborg elaborated it beyond his predecessors, and beyond our ability to follow. To him also **is now ascribed** the nebular theory of the solar system, and the position of this system in the visible universe. In his *Principia* is to be found an elaborate, and, we are persuaded, true theory of phenomena of light and of electricity or magnetism, with calculation of coming variations of the magnetic needle for a century. We are not at the end of his philosophic and inventive anticipations, the correctness of which may serve to give confidence that even in these pursuits Swedenborg was being led in the path of truth. But after he found himself engaged in his true mission of unfolding the genuine meaning of the Scriptures, he made no attempt to display his discoveries in science or philosophy, regarding all the insight he had obtained into the mysteries of creation as a training and basis for understanding the mysteries of the Divine providence in the care of human souls.

Of the other two volumes of the *Opera Philosophica et Mineralia*, on Iron and on Copper, there is little to be said of general interest, since they are practical treatises on the mining and working of these metals. In his own preface Swedenborg says —

"I intend to distribute the treatise upon each

STUDIES AND PUBLICATIONS ABROAD

metal, as here upon iron, into three divisions. The first division will comprise in particular the processes and methods of smelting that are in use in various parts of Europe; and as the methods in vogue in Sweden have come more under my own observation than those employed in other countries, so I dwell upon them longer in proportion. The second division will give the various methods of assaying; by which the ore is tried in small fires, or assaying furnaces, and its composition examined, in order that it may be the better proceeded with on a large scale. The third division will embrace an account of all the different chemical processes that have fallen under my notice, with the characteristics of each; and will deliver numerous experiments and observations which have been made on one and the same metal in the course of solution, crystallization, precipitation, and other chemical changes."

The great learning and practical value of the volumes on metallurgy was at once admitted. The Academy of Sciences at Paris translated and published the treatise on Iron. In England the work was cited as of the highest authority. In Russia its author was elected corresponding mem-

the nebular theory of the solar system, and the position of this system in the visible universe. In his *Principia* is to be found an elaborate, and, we are persuaded, true theory of phenomena of light and of electricity or magnetism, with calculation of coming variations of the magnetic needle for a century. We are not at the end of his philosophic and inventive anticipations, the correctness of which may serve to give confidence that even in these pursuits Swedenborg was being led in the path of truth. But after he found himself engaged in his true mission of unfolding the genuine meaning of the Scriptures, he made no attempt to display his discoveries in science or philosophy, regarding all the insight he had obtained into the mysteries of creation as a training and basis for understanding the mysteries of the Divine providence in the care of human souls.

Of the other two volumes of the *Opera Philosophica et Mineralia*, on Iron and on Copper, there is little to be said of general interest, since they are practical treatises on the mining and working of these metals. In his own preface Swedenborg says —

"I intend to distribute the treatise upon each

STUDIES AND PUBLICATIONS ABROAD

metal, as here upon iron, into three divisions. The first division will comprise in particular the processes and methods of smelting that are in use in various parts of Europe; and as the methods in vogue in Sweden have come more under my own observation than those employed in other countries, so I dwell upon them longer in proportion. The second division will give the various methods of assaying; by which the ore is tried in small fires, or assaying furnaces, and its composition examined, in order that it may be the better proceeded with on a large scale. The third division will embrace an account of all the different chemical processes that have fallen under my notice, with the characteristics of each; and will deliver numerous experiments and observations which have been made on one and the same metal in the course of solution, crystallization, precipitation, and other chemical changes."

The great learning and practical value of the volumes on metallurgy was at once admitted. The Academy of Sciences at Paris translated and published the treatise on Iron. In England the work was cited as of the highest authority. In Russia its author was elected corresponding member of the Imperial Academy of Sciences; and at home he became Fellow of the Royal Academy of Sciences. Fifty years after its publication, on the report of a commission to the unfortunate Louis XV, that there did not yet exist any theory of the magnet, the Marquis de Thome responded indignantly and at length, declaring that the *Opera Philosophica* of Swedenborg was held in high esteem in all Europe, and that the most celebrated men "had not disdained to draw materials from it to assist them in their labors;" that "the theory of the Swedish author is a true theory of the magnet, and of all magnetism;" and that M. Camus, who performed such surprising things with the magnet before their eyes, admitted that he had "derived from this author almost all the knowledge he exhibited on the subject." To this we may add that some practical electricians of the present day are finding in this theory explanations of results which they do not find explained by any other.

For completing the publication of the *Opera Mineralia et Philosophica* Swedenborg obtained an extension of his leave of absence, but in July, 1734, was in his seat again, examining candidates

STUDIES AND PUBLICATIONS ABROAD

for the post of Assay Master, and was constant in attendance till the middle of January, 1736, when he requested the Royal leave to attend the burial of his father in West Gothland. But these practical duties of the College of Mines could not long satisfy his aspirations for the advancement of human knowledge, and in the following May he again petitioned King Frederic to grant him three or four years' leave of absence, on half pay, for the elaboration and publishing of works he had undertaken requiring "long and deep thought and a mind unencumbered with cares and troubles." This request was referred by the King to the Royal College and received its approval, whereupon Swedenborg thanked the College, and especially for the continuance of half his salary "in consideration partly of the well-intentioned and useful design I have in view, and partly because I have been an Assessor in the Royal College for twenty years. It will both cheer me on and be an assistance in my proposed undertaking, which will be sufficiently expensive."

On the 3d of July he took his leave of their Majesties, who were very gracious, and on the 10th of the Royal College, to which he did not

EMANUEL SWEDENBORG

return till November, 1740. Proceeding to Hamburg he called on Pastor Christopher Wolf with letters from Benzelius, as we learn from a letter of Wolf's to Benzelius, dated Sept. 1, 1736:—

"I received recently your most welcome letter, which was handed to me by your relative, the most noble Swedenborg, who was known to me by name already. I value his most celebrated work in mineralogy so much the more, because in the present age scarcely any one can be compared with this most excellent and clear-headed man in this department."

Of this and other journeys and sojourns in foreign lands we have many notes of his own hand, mentioning places, persons, churches, and libraries visited, with interesting comments on the manners and customs of the people, and with an occasional remark on what he then had in hand. It was no longer metallurgy and the material elements that he was studying, but man — body, mind, and soul — and his relation to the Supreme Being. For some years he had given close attention to the study of Anatomy, and to this he now devoted several years' labor, yet with the soul always in view. Already in September

STUDIES AND PUBLICATIONS ABROAD

in Paris he notes, "I made the first draught of the introduction to my new treatise [Economy of the Animal Kingdom], namely, that the soul of wisdom is the knowledge and acknowledgment of the Supreme Being." Here in Paris and in Italy he found the best opportunities for anatomical studies, and in Amsterdam for printing his *Œconomia Regni Animalis*, on the completion of which he returned home in November, 1740. This quarto volume of 582 pages represents, however, but a small part of the author's labors during these four years Very much more is contained in the great pile of notes, observations, and deductions which he brought home in manuscript, from which important treatises have since been and are still being published.

Not simple phenomena, but their hidden causes Swedenborg was always seeking. The philosophy of his century was leading to negative results, to disbelief in the power of reason to conclude anything in regard to the Divine Being, however clear to moral sense may be His existence. Kant's results, as summed up by Lewes, are these:—

"The attempt to demonstrate the existence of God is an impossible attempt. Reason is utterly

EMANUEL SWEDENBORG

incompetent to the task. The attempt to penetrate the essence of things — to know things *per se* — to know *noumena* — is also an impossible attempt. And yet that God exists, that the World exists, are irresistible convictions. There is another certitude, therefore, besides that derived from demonstration, and this is moral certitude, which is grounded upon belief. I cannot say, 'It is morally certain that God exists,' but I must say, 'I am morally certain that God exists.'"[1]

Swedenborg himself wrote in his *Principia* —

"When therefore the philosopher has arrived at the end of his studies, even supposing him to have acquired so complete a knowledge of all mundane things that nothing more remains for him to learn, he must there stop; for he can never know the nature of the Infinite Being, of His Supreme Intelligence, Supreme Providence, Supreme Love, Supreme Justice, and other infinite attributes. He will therefore acknowledge that in respect to this supremely intelligent and wise Being his knowledge is nothing: he will hence most profoundly venerate Him with the utmost devotion of soul; so that at the mere

[1] LEWES: *History of Philosophy*, ii, 518.

STUDIES AND PUBLICATIONS ABROAD

thought of Him his whole frame, or membranous and sensitive system, will awfully, yet sweetly tremble, from the inmost to the outermost principles of its being."

But in the same year with the *Principia* Swedenborg had continued his investigation of the questions of his time in his Sketch of a Philosophical Argument on the Infinite and the Final Cause of Creation; and on the Intercourse between the Soul and the Body. In this essay his unswerving faith in Revelation is conspicuous all through, and with it a recognition of something higher than merely natural reason. In the Preface he says —

"Philosophy if it be truly rational can never be contrary to Revelation. . . . The end of reason can be no other than that man may perceive the things that are revealed and those that are created: thus the rational cannot be contrary to the Divine, since the end why reason is given us is that we may be empowered to perceive that there is a God and to know that He is to be worshipped. If reason be the mean, endowed with the faculty and power of perceiving, and if the actual perception be the end, then the mean, in so far as it is correctly rational, cannot be repugnant to the end. The very mysteries that are above reason cannot be contrary to reason, although reason is unable to explain their grounds." Thus begins the first chapter: —

"In order that we may be favored and happy in our endeavors, they must begin from the Infinite, or God, without whom no undertakings can attain a prosperous issue. He it is that bestows on all things their principles; from whom all things finite took their rise; from whom we have our souls, and by whom we live; by whom we are at once mortals and immortals; to whom in fine we owe everything. And as the soul was created by Him and added to the body, and reason to both, in order that the soul might be His, so our thoughts, whether we revolve them within, or utter them in words, or commit them to writing, must always be so directed as to have their beginning and end from Him; whereby the Deity may be present with gracious favor as the First and the Last, in either end as well as in the means."

Then alluding to the desire of human reason to be convinced in order to accept theology, he shows at length the impossibility of the reason's

STUDIES AND PUBLICATIONS ABROAD

concluding anything in regard to the nature of the Infinite, by comparison with the finite. But, not abandoning the matter so, he proceeds to inquire as to the producing cause of what is finite, even of its first and least particular. Showing that it cannot have its existence of itself, nor of any other finite thing, since then the question would be removed but one step backward, he concludes that reason must admit an infinite producing cause. But of these there cannot be many, only One. Now taking this Infinite as the cause of all creation, he deduces the entire variety from the same Cause, in all its intricacy and order. Then citing examples of this order and intricate beauty — especially in ample detail from the construction and operation of the organs of the human body — calling forth our admiration, he seeks to transfer this and transform it into adoration for the Deity. But this full acknowledgment, he admits, must come partly on self-evidence, springing from the human soul, and partly as a consequence from the arguments adduced.

"There is in fact," he says, "a tacit consent, or a tacit conclusion of the soul, to the being as well as to the infinity of God. This is dictated, I say, partly by the soul in its own free essence, partly by the soul as instructed and advised by the diverse innumerable effects presented in the world. . . . It cannot be denied that there is that in man as man, provided he enjoy the use of reason, which acknowledges an omnipotent God, an omnipresent and all-provident Deity; it seems therefore to be innate, and to be a power or action of reason, when not on the one hand troubled too much by its own ideas, nor on the other hand too destitute of all cultivation and development. But we care not whether it be spontaneous or the contrary, if it be admitted that there is no one living, provided he be not over or under rational, but acknowledges the existence of a Deity, however ignorant he be of the Divine nature. Hence it is that after man has exerted his powers and whetted his reason to find out this nature, he falls into strange darkness and ideal conclusions. He knows indeed that there is a Deity, that there is an omnipotence, but he has been unsuccessful in eliciting the nature of either from any dictates of reason. . . . In truth mankind is always desirous to imagine the qualities of God, to bring Him within the bounds of rea-

STUDIES AND PUBLICATIONS ABROAD

son and rational ideas, and to finite and fix Him in something, by something, or to something. For this reason the above investigation has all along been the issue and offspring of reason and philosophy. And though the philosophers have heard that He is infinite, yet on behalf of poor reason, which is always bounded by finite limits, they imagine the infinite as finite, being unable to perceive at all apart from the finite. We now therefore see why reason has failed, and that the cause is the same in the common people as in the learned."

Proceeding then to point out in detail the errors of many theories, all of which are owing to the judging of the Infinite from the finite, he concludes that —

"Beyond our finite sphere there are verily infinities, to the knowledge of which it is useless to aspire, and which in the Infinite are infinitely many and can be known to no one but the Infinite. In order that these may in some measure be conceived by the soul introduced through faith into communion with the Infinite, it has pleased God to discover by Revelation much whereby the mind can finitely conceive and express Him: not how-

say, partly by the soul in its own free essence, partly by the soul as instructed and advised by the diverse innumerable effects presented in the world. . . . It cannot be denied that there is that in man as man, provided he enjoy the use of reason, which acknowledges an omnipotent God, an omnipresent and all-provident Deity; it seems therefore to be innate, and to be a power or action of reason, when not on the one hand troubled too much by its own ideas, nor on the other hand too destitute of all cultivation and development. But we care not whether it be spontaneous or the contrary, if it be admitted that there is no one living, provided he be not over or under rational, but acknowledges the existence of a Deity, however ignorant he be of the Divine nature. Hence it is that after man has exerted his powers and whetted his reason to find out this nature, he falls into strange darkness and ideal conclusions. He knows indeed that there is a Deity, that there is an omnipotence, but he has been unsuccessful in eliciting the nature of either from any dictates of reason. . . . In truth mankind is always desirous to imagine the qualities of God, to bring Him within the bounds of rea-

STUDIES AND PUBLICATIONS ABROAD

son and rational ideas, and to finite and fix Him in something, by something, or to something. For this reason the above investigation has all along been the issue and offspring of reason and philosophy. And though the philosophers have heard that He is infinite, yet on behalf of poor reason, which is always bounded by finite limits, they imagine the infinite as finite, being unable to perceive at all apart from the finite. We now therefore see why reason has failed, and that the cause is the same in the common people as in the learned."

Proceeding then to point out in detail the errors of many theories, all of which are owing to the judging of the Infinite from the finite, he concludes that —

"Beyond our finite sphere there are verily infinities, to the knowledge of which it is useless to aspire, and which in the Infinite are infinitely many and can be known to no one but the Infinite. In order that these may in some measure be conceived by the soul introduced through faith into communion with the Infinite, it has pleased God to discover by Revelation much whereby the mind can finitely conceive and express Him: not however that finite perceptions or expressions are similar or adequate to Him, but only that those made use of are not repugnant."

Returning to what has been granted, that the Infinite exists as the cause of the finite world, Swedenborg next questions whether or no there must be a *nexus*, or means of influence, between the Infinite and the finite. Showing by argument that a *nexus* is indispensable, he then shows that the *nexus* itself must be infinite, not finite. Assuming this to be within our knowledge by proof of reason, he asks whether if any one can tell us more about this *nexus* that shall agree with what we already know, we shall not listen to it. And then he alleges, what he says has been taught by Revelation, that this *nexus* is the Son of God, begotten from eternity,[1] to be the means of communication from the Infinite with the finite. But, from what he has already shown, he declares this *nexus* itself to be infinite; and as there cannot be two infinites, the *nexus*, or the Son of God, is none other than the Infinite, God Himself.

[1] This current theological expression was firmly repudiated in his later works, in which he recognized the Son as the Divine Presence in humanity, thus in *time*.

STUDIES AND PUBLICATIONS ABROAD

"To say then," he continues, "that the finite came forth mediately through the Son, is exactly tantamount to saying that it came forth immediately through the Father, or immediately through the Son; since the Father and Son are alike the Infinite, and the Infinite is the immediate cause of the finite." Then showing that in creation there must be a Divine, or infinite, final end; that this end is to be reached through the whole chain of creation, of which man is the last link, the crown of all, he declares that in man therefore for the fulfilment of the Divine end, there must be something that can partake of the Infinite:—

"Not certainly in the fact that man is an animal and has senses provided him to enjoy the delights of the world; nor in the fact that he has a soul, for his soul is finite and can contain nothing of the Infinite. Neither in reason, which is the effect of the coöperation between the soul and the body; which, as they are both finite, so the effect of both is also finite: therefore it does not lie in reason. So far we find nothing Divine in man. Where is that, then, which appears to be nowhere, and yet is necessary to realize the Divine end? . . It lies in this, that man can acknowledge and does acknowledge God; that he can believe and does believe that God is infinite; that though he is ignorant of the nature of the Deity, yet he can acknowledge and does acknowledge His existence, and this without the shadow of doubt. And especially does it consist in this further privilege, that by this undoubting faith he is sensible in love, or delight resulting from love, of a peculiar connection with the Infinite. But where he doubts, he does not acknowledge and the Divine is not in him. All Divine worship proceeds from this fountain of faith and love. . . . Thus the true divinity in man, who is the final effect in which the Divine end dwells, is none other than an acknowledgment of the existence and infinity of God . . . and a sense of delight in the love of God, although human reason cannot do this of itself, inasmuch as man, with all his parts and his very soul, is finite; notwithstanding which he may be a fit recipient, and as he is in the finite sphere he may concur to dispose himself for reception."

Now comes the crowning effort in this argument. It being granted that the Divine sought this final return of creation to Itself, the question is asked, how it is to be secured through the va-

STUDIES AND PUBLICATIONS ABROAD

rious stages from first to last. The answer being given that it is to be secured by means of the soul, which from its altitude is designed to rule the body, it is asked by what means the true order is to be restored when, as must have been foreseen, the body refuses to obey the instincts of the soul and fails to serve its true purpose. And the triumphant answer is given that "God provided against this by His Infinite, only-begotten Son, who took on Him the ultimate effect of the world, or a manhood and a human shape, and thereby was infinite in and with the finite, and consequently restored the *nexus* in His own person between the Infinite and the finite, so that the primary end was realized. . . . The Infinite . . . thus Himself became the last effect — at once God and man, the Mediator between the finite and the Infinite. . . . Without Him there would be no connection between the last effect and the Infinite; whereas through Him somewhat of the Divine may dwell in us, namely, in the faculty to know and believe that there is a God, and that He is infinite. And again through Him, by the use of the means, we are led to true religion, and become children of God, and not of the world."

EMANUEL SWEDENBORG

Observing now that this is not the place to explain the nature of the connection by the *nexus*, he stops to consider the difficulty which may be felt as to the condition of those who have not learned and believed in the Messiah. He concludes that though the coming of the Messiah is the essential means of salvation, yet "those who did not know and do not know that He has come, could and can become partakers by the grace of God through His coming; for otherwise we should suppose something in God that would seem at variance with His Divine nature and end. But as for those who know the Messiah, or have the opportunity to know Him, we say that they too are made partakers through His coming; but the knowledge also of His coming is necessary to them in order to their faith, for the quality of faith is determined by knowledge, and its perception rendered distinct and full; and therefore where knowledge is given, it and faith are inseparable."

The summing up of our author's argument is as follows: "Observe what we have gained. We have the affirmation of reason for the existence of God, and also for His Infinity; and as this is

STUDIES AND PUBLICATIONS ABROAD

now positive knowledge, together with that other truth of the existence of a *nexus* between God and man in the Person of the only-begotten Son, so we may legitimately advance, not indeed to inquire into the nature or qualities of Deity, because He is infinite, and His qualities therefore we can never penetrate, but to inquire what there can be in man to lead to this primary end; what there can be in him that does not repugn the infinite and the *nexus;* how a confessedly infinite Deity may best be expressed in finite terms that shall not be repugnant to the occasion; what befitting worship consists in; what is the peculiar efficacy of faith proceeding from a true acknowledgment of God; with innumerable other subjects, which cannot be settled briefly, but require to be rationally deduced in a volume by themselves. And as by the grace of God we have all these matters revealed in Holy Scripture, so where reason is perplexed in its apprehensions we must at once have recourse to Revelation; and where we cannot discover from Revelation either what we should adopt or in what sense we should understand its declarations, we must then fly to the oracle of reason."

V

CONTINUED STUDY OF THE BODY IN SEARCH OF THE SOUL

WHAT is our quest? A man fitted by birthright and by training of heart and mind to recognize the sign of the Son of Man in the clouds of perverted Scripture, that have darkened human reason and withdrawn the light of faith. And here we have Emanuel Swedenborg of such birthright, with devotion of his life to the advancement of mankind, led through severest mathematical, mechanical, and philosophical reasoning — without as yet any consciousness of special guidance or purpose — to absolute demonstration in his own mind of the necessity and the existence of the Divine Son of Man, to be sought and found by us in the Holy Scriptures. But let us wait. Scientific and philosophic studies are not yet completed. Twelve years more are to be devoted to them before the mission is Divinely signified to him of revealing this Son of Man in His Word.

The Economy of the Animal Kingdom, pub-

IN SEARCH OF THE SOUL

lished in 1740, was an attempt to reach a philosophic view of the human organism as the abode and instrument of the soul. Of his method the author says —

"In the experimental knowledge of anatomy our way has been pointed out by men of the greatest and most cultivated talents, such as Eustachius [and nineteen others named], whose discoveries, far from consisting of fallacious, vague, and empty speculations, will forever continue to be of practical use to posterity. Assisted by the studies and elaborate writings of these illustrious men and fortified by their authority, I have resolved to commence and complete my design — that is to say, to open some part of those things which it is generally supposed that nature has involved in obscurity. Here and there I have taken the liberty to throw in the results of my own experience; but this only sparingly, for on deeply considering the matter I deemed it best to make use of the facts supplied by others. Indeed, there are some that seem born for experimental observation and endowed with a sharper insight than others, as if they possessed naturally a finer acumen. . . . There are others again who enjoy

EMANUEL SWEDENBORG

a natural faculty for contemplating facts already discovered, and eliciting their causes. Both are peculiar gifts and are seldom united in the same person. Besides, I found when intently occupied in exploring the secrets of the human body that as soon as I discovered anything which had not been observed before, I began, seduced probably by self-love, to grow blind to the most acute lucubrations and researches of others, and to originate the whole series of inductive arguments from my particular discovery alone. . . , Nay, when I essayed to form principles from these discoveries, I thought I could detect in various other phenomena much to confirm their truth, although in reality they were fairly susceptible of no construction of the kind. I therefore laid aside my instruments, and restraining my desire for making observations, determined rather to rely on the researches of others than to trust to my own."

After describing as from experience the faculty which some enjoy — who ever more than he? — of confining their attention to one thing and evolving with distinctness all that lies in it, of distributing their thoughts into classes separat-

IN SEARCH OF THE SOUL

ing mixed topics into appropriate divisions, of skilfully subordinating the series thus divided, and of being never overwhelmed by the multiplicity of things, but continually enlightened more and more, he says of such as enjoy the faculty —

"The fictitious depresses them, the obscure pains them; but they are exhilarated by the truth, and in the presence of everything that is clear they too are clear and serene. When after a long course of reasoning they make a discovery of the truth, straightway there is a cheering light and joyful confirmatory brightness that plays around the sphere of their mind, and a kind of mysterious radiation — I know not whence it proceeds — that darts through some sacred temple in the brain. Thus a sort of rational instinct displays itself, and in a manner gives notice that the soul is called into a state of inward communion, and has returned at that moment into the golden age of its intellectual perfections. The mind that has known this pleasure is wholly carried away in pursuit of it; and in the kindling flame of its love despises in comparison, as external pastimes, all merely corporeal pleasures; and though it recognizes them as means for exciting the animal mind

EMANUEL SWEDENBORG

and the purer blood, it on no account follows them as ends. Persons of this cast regard the arts and sciences only as aids to wisdom, and learn them as helps to its attainment, not that they may be reputed wise for possessing them. They modestly restrain all tendency to inflated ideas of themselves, knowing that the sciences are an ocean of which they can catch but a few drops. They look on no one with a scornful brow or supercilious air, nor arrogate any praise to themselves. They ascribe all to the Deity, and regard Him as the source from which all true wisdom descends. In the promotion of His glory they place the end and object of their own."

Remarking now how sensual and worldly cares impair this noble faculty, he says, "Nothing superinduces more darkness on the human mind than the interference of its own fancied providence in matters that properly belong to the Divine providence." And then he goes on to say, still as from experience —

"This faculty, however, is chiefly impaired by the thirst for glory and the love of self. I know not what darkness overspreads the rational faculties when the mind begins to swell with pride,

IN SEARCH OF THE SOUL

or when our intuition of objects calls up in the objects themselves the image and glory of our own selfhood. It is like pouring a liquor upon some exquisite wine, which throws it into a froth, sullies its purity, and clouds its translucence. It is as if the animal spirits were stirred into waves, and a tempest drove the grosser blood into insurgent motion, by which the organs of internal sensation or perception becoming swollen, the powers of thought are dulled, and the whole scene of action in their theatre changed. In those who experience these disorderly states, the rational faculty is crippled and brought to a standstill; or rather its movements become retrograde instead of progressive. A limit is put to its operations, which its possessor imagines to be the limit of all human capacity, because he himself is unable to overstep it. He sees little or nothing in the most studied researches of others, but everything — oh, how vain-glorious! — in his own. Nor can he return to correct conceptions until his elated thoughts have subsided to their proper level. 'There are many,' says Seneca, 'who might have attained wisdom, had they not fancied they had attained it already.' The Muses love a tranquil mind; and there is nothing but humility, contempt of self, and simple love of truth, that can prevent or remedy the evils we have described.

"But how often does a man labor in vain to divest himself of his own nature! How often, when ignorant or unmindful of the love that creeps upon him, will he betray a partiality to himself and the offspring of his own genius! If an author therefore desires that his studies should give birth to anything of sterling value, let him be advised, when he has committed to paper what he considers to be of particular merit and is fond of frequently perusing, to lay it aside for a while, and after the lapse of months to return to it as to something he had forgotten, and as the production not of himself but of some other writer. Let him repeat this practice three or four times in the year. . . . Should his writings then often raise a blush upon his countenance, should he no longer feel an overweening confidence with regard to the lines which had received the latest polish from his hands, let him be assured that he has made some little progress in wisdom."

At the conclusion of Part First, Swedenborg gives a chapter which he styles An Introduction

IN SEARCH OF THE SOUL

to Rational Psychology, regarding this as the first and last of those sciences which lead to the knowledge of the animal economy. "But whereas the soul," he goes on to say, "lives withdrawn so far within that she cannot be exposed to view until the coverings under which she is hidden are unfolded and removed in order, it hence becomes necessary that we ascend to her by the same steps or degrees and the same ladder by which her nature in the formation of the things of her kingdom descends into her body. By way therefore of an Introduction to Rational Psychology, I will premise the Doctrine of Series and Degrees — a doctrine of which in the preceding chapters I have made such frequent mention, the design of which is to teach the nature of order and its rules as observed and prescribed in the succession of things."

The first chapter of Part Second is devoted to the motion of the brain, the second to the cortical substance of the brain, and the third to the human soul. Confessing the difficulties in the search for the soul and his frequent disappointments, he says —

"At length I awoke as from a deep sleep when I discovered that nothing is farther removed from the human understanding than what at the same time is really present to it; and that nothing is more present to it than what is universal, prior, and superior, since this enters into every particular and into everything posterior and inferior. What is more omnipresent than the Deity — in whom we live and move and have our being — and yet what is more remote from the sphere of the understanding?

"The more any one is perfected in judgment, and the better he discerns the distinctions of things, the more clearly will he perceive that there is an order in things, that there are degrees of order, and that it is by these alone he can progress, and this step by step from the lowest sphere to the highest, or from the outermost to the innermost. For as often as Nature ascends away from external phenomena, or betakes herself inward, she seems to have separated from us, and to have left us altogether in the dark as to what direction she has taken. We have need therefore of some science to serve as our guide in tracing out her steps, to arrange all things into series, to distinguish these series into degrees, and to contemplate the order of each thing in the order of

IN SEARCH OF THE SOUL

the whole. The science which does this I call the Doctrine of Series and Degrees, or the Doctrine of Order . . . [which] teaches the distinction and relation between things superior and inferior, or prior and posterior. . . .

"I am strongly persuaded that the essence and nature of the soul, its influx into the body, and the reciprocal action of the body can never come to demonstration without these doctrines, combined with a knowledge of anatomy, pathology, and psychology; nay, even of physics, and especially of the auras of the world. . . . This and no other is the reason that with diligent study and intense application I have investigated the anatomy of the body, and principally the human, so far as it is known from experience; and that I have followed the anatomy of all its parts, in the same manner as I have here investigated the cortical substance."

The soul itself and a society of souls he finds to be the final purpose of all creation, and then he concludes —

"If there be a society of souls, must not the City of God on the universal earth be the seminary of it? The most universal law of its citizens is, that they love their neighbor as themselves, and God more than themselves. All other things are means, and are good in proportion as they lead directly to this end. Now as everything in the universe is created as a means to this end, it follows that the application of the means, and a true regard of the end in the means, are the sole constituents of a citizen [of the Holy City]. The Holy Scripture is the code of rules for obtaining the end by the means.

"These rules are not so dark or obscure as the philosophy of the mind and the love of self and of the world would make them; nor so deep and hidden but that any sincere soul which permits the Spirit of God to govern it may draw them from this pure fountain — pure enough for the use and service of the members of the City of God all over the world — without violating any form of ecclesiastical government. It is foretold that the kingdom of God shall come; that at last the guests shall be assembled at the marriage supper; that the wolf shall lie down with the lamb, the leopard with the kid, the lion with the ox; that the young child shall play with the asp; that the mountain of God shall rise above all other moun-

IN SEARCH OF THE SOUL

tains, and that the Gentile and the stranger shall come to it to pay their worship."

To quote more from this remarkable work of the Economy of the Animal Kingdom would exceed the proper limits of this small volume. Of the literary merits of the work S. T. Coleridge said — " I remember nothing in Lord Bacon superior, few passages equal, either in depth of thought, or in richness, dignity, and felicity of diction, or in the weightiness of the truths contained."[1] And Dr. Spurgin, formerly President of the Royal College of Physicians in London, pronounced the Part on the Soul "a production unparalleled for excellence in the whole compass of human philosophy."[2]

But with the preparation and printing of the Economy of the Animal Kingdom in 1740 and 1741, Swedenborg's studies in this direction were by no means at an end. Though he returned to his duties in the Royal College in November, 1740, fulfilling these duties anew for two years and a half, he had already prescribed for himself a

[1] *Literary Remains*, May 27, 1827.
[2] *Wisdom, Intelligence, and Science the True Characteristics of Emanuel Swedenborg.*

EMANUEL SWEDENBORG

definite series of continued studies, year by year, to be completed in 1747 with that of "The City of God." These studies had been pursued with such diligence that in June, 1743, he petitioned the King and the Royal College for a new leave of absence, that he might go abroad and complete and see through the press a new work of not less than five hundred sheets. Leave having been obtained, Swedenborg repaired to Holland to consult the chief libraries and then to print a portion of what he had prepared, in two quarto volumes of 438 and 486 pages, entitled *Regnum Animale* — The Animal Kingdom. In his Prologue to the first volume he said —

"Not very long since I published the Economy of the Animal Kingdom . . . and before traversing the whole field in detail, I made a rapid passage to the soul and put forth an essay respecting it. But on considering the matter more deeply, I found that I had directed my course thither both too hastily and too fast — after having explored the blood only and its peculiar organs. I took the step impelled by an ardent desire for knowledge."

Now he proposes to traverse the whole kingdom of the body, hoping that by bending his

IN SEARCH OF THE SOUL

course inward continually he may open all the doors that lead to her and at length by the Divine permission contemplate the soul herself. But he supposes the objection made that "all those things which transcend our present state are matters for faith and not for intellect;" that the intellect should be "contented with this its lot, and not aspire to higher things which, inasmuch as they are sanctuaries and matters of Revelation, exist to faith only.... Where there is faith what need is there of demonstration?... Faith is above all demonstration because it is above all the philosophy of the human mind." His reply is, "I grant this; nor would I persuade any one who comprehends these high truths by faith, to attempt to comprehend them by his intellect: let him abstain from my books. Whoso believes Revelation implicitly, without consulting the intellect, is the happiest of mortals, the nearest to heaven, and at once a native of both worlds. But these pages of mine are written with a view to those only who never believe anything but what they can receive with the intellect; consequently who boldly invalidate and are fain to deny the existence of all supereminent things, sublimer than themselves —

EMANUEL SWEDENBORG

as the soul itself, and what follows therefrom; **its** life, immortality, heaven, etc. ... Consequently they honor and worship nature, the world, and themselves; in other respects they compare themselves to brutes, and think that they shall die in the same manner as brutes, and their souls exhale and evaporate: thus they rush fearlessly into wickedness. For these persons only I am anxious; and, as I said before, for them I indite and to them I dedicate my work. For when I shall have demonstrated truths themselves by the analytic method, I hope that those debasing shadows or material clouds which darken the sacred temple of the mind will be dispersed; and that thus at last under the favor of God, who is the Sun of Wisdom, an access will be opened and a way laid down to faith. **My** ardent desire and zeal for this end is what urges and animates me."

In the Second Part he says —

"If we wish to invite real truths, whether natural or moral or spiritual — for they all make common cause by means of correspondence and representation — into the sphere of our rational minds, it is necessary that we **extinguish the impure fires** of the body and thereby our **own delu-**

IN SEARCH OF THE SOUL

sive lights, and submit and allow our minds unmolested by the influences of the body to be illumined with the rays of the spiritual power: then for the first time truths flow in, for they all emanate from that power as their peculiar fountain. Nor when they are present, are there wanting a multitude of signs by which they attest themselves — namely, the varied forms of sweetness and delight attendant upon truth attained, and affecting the mind as the enjoyments that result from the harmonies of external objects affect the lower and sensitive faculties of the body: for as soon as ever a truth shines forth, such a mind exults and rejoices; and this joy is the ground of its first assent, and of its first delighted smile. But the actual confirmation of the truth proceeds from its accordance with numerous reasons, confirmed by experience by means of the sciences, and each point of which accordance receives a similar assent — the mind going onward the while with assiduous attention and pains by the analytic way, or from effects to causes. In addition to these delights there are still more universal signs, as the desire and the passion for attaining truth, and the love of the truth attained, not for the sake of our own advantage, but for that of the advantage of human society; and neither for the glory of ourselves or of society, but of the Supreme Divinity alone. This is the only way to truths: other things as means, which are infinite, God Omnipotent provides."

Inquiring then into the ends or purposes of the provision by which it is ordained that man should ascend from lowest and outermost to highest and innermost, he unfolds them comprehensively, concluding with these — "that in this ultimate circle of nature we may receive the wonders of the world, and as we ascend the steps and ladders of intelligence receive still greater wonders, in all their significance and with full vision; and that at length we may comprehend by faith those profound miracles that cannot be comprehended by the intellect; and from all these things, in the deep hush of awe and amazement, venerate and adore the omnipotence and providence of the Supreme Creator; and thus in the contemplation of Him regard as vanity everything that we leave behind us. . . . The last end, which also is the first, is that our minds, at length become

IN SEARCH OF THE SOUL

forms of intelligence and innocence, may constitute a spiritual heaven, a kingdom of God, or a holy society, in which the end of creation may be regarded by God, and by which God may be regarded as the end of ends. From infinite wisdom, added to equal power, and this to equal providence, such perpetual end flows constantly from the first end to the last, and from the last to the first, through the intermediate ends, that declare the glory of the Divinity." To this he adds in a note, "I shall treat of these subjects, by the blessing of God, in the last of my analytic Parts. But as yet we are dwelling in the mere effects of the world, which exhibit the amazing and Divine circle of these ends before the contemplation of our very senses."

Of the high purposes and original method pursued in this treatise on The Animal Kingdom, the following extracts will give a good idea:—

"As the blood is continually making its circle of life, that is to say, is in a constant revolution of birth and death; as it dies in its old age and is regenerated or born anew; and as the veins solicitously gather together the whole of its corporeal part, and the lymphatics of its spirituous

EMANUEL SWEDENBORG

part, and successively bring it back, refect it with new chyle, and restore it to the pure and youthful blood; and as the kidneys constantly purge it of impurities, and restore its pure parts to the blood, so likewise man, who lives at once in body and spirit while he lives in the blood, must undergo the same fortunes generally, and in the progress of his regeneration must daily do the like. Such a perpetual symbolical representation is there of spiritual life in corporeal life; as likewise a perpetual typical representation of the soul in the body. In this consists the searching of the heart and the reins, which is a thing purely Divine.

"In our Doctrine of Representations and Correspondences, we shall treat of both these symbolical and typical representations, and of the astonishing things which occur, I will not say in the living body only, but throughout nature, and which correspond so entirely to supreme and spiritual things that one would swear that the physical world is purely symbolical of the spiritual world, insomuch that if we choose to express any natural truth in physical and definite vocal terms, and to convert these terms only into the corresponding spiritual terms, we shall by this means elicit a

IN SEARCH OF THE SOUL

spiritual truth or theological dogma, in place of the physical truth or precept; although no mortal would have predicted that anything of the kind could possibly arise by bare literal transposition, inasmuch as the one precept, considered separately from the other, appears to have absolutely no relation to it.

"I intend hereafter to communicate a number of examples of such correspondences, together with a vocabulary containing the terms of spiritual things, as well as of the physical things for which they are to be substituted. This symbolism pervades the living body; and I have chosen simply to indicate it here, for the purpose of pointing out the spiritual meaning of searching the reins."

In addition to what Swedenborg himself published of The Animal Kingdom, several parts have been recently published in Germany and England, including three thick octavo volumes on "The Brain, Considered Anatomically, Physiologically, and Philosophically."[1] That so much labor was given to the study of the brain was doubtless because the author found in it the seat

[1] JAMES SPIERS: London, 1882, 1887.

of the soul, to knowledge of which he was aspiring. In the Animal Kingdom he says —

"*The soul is properly the universal essence of its body*. The soul is the only thing substantial and essential in its body. From it are derived and born all the substances and essences which are called composite and corporeal. For what can truly be unless it be from a thing prior, more simple, and more unique, which is the beginning of the rest? That which gives to others being and existence must itself be. It cannot be produced from modes, accidents, and qualities without a subject and form, and consequently without a real essence and substance. The soul also is peculiar or individual, and there is not one universal soul for all; so that the soul of one cannot belong to the body of another; for — which is to be demonstrated — the very form of the body is the result of its essential determination, or the body itself represents the soul as it were in an image. . . . The higher or highest universal essence is the soul, the lower is the animal spirit, and the third the blood. The highest essence imparts being, the power of acting and life, to the lower, and this imparts the same in like manner to

IN SEARCH OF THE SOUL

the lowest; the lowest, consequently, exists and subsists from the first by means of the middle. . . . The determinations of the highest universal essence of the bodily system are those fibres which are the simplest of all, and which are like rays of the soul, and the first designations of forms. The determinations of the lower universal essence are those fibres which are derived from the most simple; but those of the lowest are the arterial and venous vessels. As the essences, so also the determinations are in turn derived from one another, the higher imparting being to the lower. From these determinations, or from these determining essences, all the organic viscera, and consequently the whole bodily system, is woven and formed."

"*It is the cerebrum through which the intercourse between the soul and the body is established; for it is as it were the link and the uniting medium.* From what follows it will appear that the soul is in the cerebrum as it were in its heaven and Olympus, though it is essentially everywhere and present in every individual part. In the cerebrum, however, is formed as it were its court and palace chamber, from which it looks around on all things belonging to it, and determines them into act in agreement with its intuition."

The thoroughness of this study of the brain with the intent to find the residence of the soul and the mode of its control over the body led to some remarkable discoveries, of which the learned world is now first becoming aware. Among these it is surprising to find the determination of the glandules of the cortical substance of the cerebrum, as the seat of the soul's sensation and control of the body. Even more surprising is Swedenborg's first general localization of the different functions of the several parts of the cerebrum. Many more observations and deductions are contained in these wonderful studies — published and unpublished — from which there is doubtless still much for students to learn. Dr. Max Newburger of Vienna in a recent essay says —

"The great physiological system set forth by Swedenborg in his two works — *Œconomia Regni Animalis* and *Regnum Animale* — contains such a number of successful anticipations of modern science that we do not wonder when we see how feebly his contemporaries grasped the true great-

IN SEARCH OF THE SOUL

ness of this Aristotle of the North. All the more strange is it, however, that the spirit of medical investigation elsewhere so lively in these times should have left untilled a field so rich as this in possibilities."[1]

In an address to the Congress of Anatomists assembled at Heidelberg, May 29, 1903, its President, Prof. Dr. Gustaf Retzius, after describing some of Swedenborg's contributions to a knowledge of the anatomy and physiology of the brain, concludes —

"Emanuel Swedenborg, therefore, according to the standpoint of his time, not only had a thorough knowledge of the construction of the brain, but had also gone far ahead of his contemporaries in fundamental questions. The question arises — how was all this possible? The answer can hardly be other than that Swedenborg was not only a learned anatomist and a sharp-sighted observer, but also in many respects an unprejudiced, acute, and deep anatomical thinker. He towers in the history of the study of the brain as a unique, wonderful, phenomenal spirit — as an ideal seeker for truth, who advanced step by step to ever

[1] *The New Philosophy*, October, 1903.

higher problems. One may more easily understand his life and labors when one places his achievements in Anatomy and Physiology in juxtaposition with those in Geology, Mechanics, Cosmogony, and Physics. With this as a background his whole endeavor becomes somewhat more intelligible. He sought to find the one principle of the universe and of life in the whole. He thought that he had found this original principle in the motion, the tremulation of the first particles. This fundamental view of things led him always further to an almost all-sided investigation and to a view of the fabric of Creation wonderfully deep for his time. With this view as a guide he gained knowledge and created theories which could be acknowledged and appreciated only in our own age."

Another section of the manuscript left by Swedenborg as a part of The Animal Kingdom, continues the study of the soul under the title of Rational Psychology:—

"All souls are purely spiritual forms. Thus all minds and their loves are purely spiritual, whether they are good or evil; for a spirit whether good or evil is still purely spirit, or purely mind, and

IN SEARCH OF THE SOUL

has purely spiritual — that is, universal — loves, in which are contained the principles of lower and purely natural loves. A good angel, as also an evil angel or devil, is purely spirit; and the loves of each are purely spiritual, but with the difference that whatever a good spirit loves, the evil spirit hates and loves its opposite.

"The first and supreme love of the spirit or soul, and the most universal, is the love of Being above itself, from which it has drawn and continually draws its essence; in which, through which, and on account of which it is and lives. This love is the first of all, because nothing can exist and subsist from itself except God, who exists in Himself, and alone is He who is. Because the soul feels this in itself, that supreme love is also inborn in it, and thus is the very Divine love within us. There is also given a love directly opposite to this, though also spiritual and supreme, which is hatred of any power or being above itself. This love is called diabolical; from it is known what the quality of good love is, and from the good what the quality of evil love is.

"The Divine providence takes especial care that individuals shall be distinct one from another, since it is the very end of creation that a most perfect society of souls may exist. . . . As then no soul is absolutely like another, but some difference or diversity of state exists between all, this has not obtained merely for the sake of distinguishing one from another, but to the end that the most perfect form of society might exist from the variety. And in such a form there must needs be not only a difference among all, but such a difference or variety as that all the individuals may come together in harmony, so as to form together a society in which nothing shall be wanting that is not found in some one. . . . This harmonic variety, however, does not consist in the outward variety of souls, but in their spiritual variety, of love toward God and toward their neighbor; for the state of the soul concerns only its spiritual state, how it may be nearest to its God. When any shade of variety is wanting, some place in heaven may be said to be as yet vacant; so that all the differences, or varieties, are to be filled up before the form can exist in full perfection.

"But whether there are to be many societies and as it were many heavens of which the uni-

IN SEARCH OF THE SOUL

versal society will consist, which is called the kingdom of God, we seem also able to conclude; for every variety, even spiritual, involves an order, with subordination and coördination. . . . For when the form of rule is most perfect, it is of necessity that all societies should produce a general harmony together, as the individual members produce a particular harmony in each society.

"This is called in heaven the kingdom of God, but on earth the seminary of that kingdom, the very city of God, which is not joined to any certain religion or church, but is distributed through the whole world; for God elects His members out of all, that is, of those who had actually loved God above themselves and their neighbors as themselves. For this is the law of all laws: in this culminate all laws, Divine and natural; all the rest are but means leading to this.

"Such a society cannot exist without its Head or Prince; that is to say, without Him who has been man, without blame and without offence, victor over all affections of the mind, virtue itself and piety itself, and the love of God above one's self, and the love of the companion and neighbor, and thus Divinity in Himself—in whom the whole society should be represented, and through whom the members of the society might come to His will. Without such a king of souls, the society might be gathered and exist in vain. This also follows necessarily from the conceded form of rule, from the difference of state of each member, and from the approach to God through love. For that form must be determined by the purer of every degree, consequently by the purest, who has been without sin, that is, by our Saviour and Preserver, Jesus Christ, in whom alone we can by faith and love draw near to the Divine throne."

We have followed Swedenborg in his search for the life and soul of the universe through the geometry and physics of the inanimate world, then through the living organism of the human body, the soul's home and body-servant, and lastly in the soul's reception of life from the Creator, in its duty to this Source of its life, and in its dependence on God-man, the Son of God, as the means of conjunction with the Divine Itself. The marked feature in all this study, that which gives its charm and inspiration, is its never-failing recognition of life, life from the Divine Life, as the cause, the essence, the form, and the activity of

IN SEARCH OF THE SOUL

each minutest entity — the living activity being manifested in inconceivably minute and rapid vibrations, or tremulations — a theory wonderfully verified in our own day, though our physicists do not yet connect the life of matter with its Source.

Yet a notable recognition of similar import in our day is that of our greatest mathematician, Professor Benjamin Pierce, who stated in the introduction to his Analytic Mechanics —

" 1. Motion is an essential element of all physical phenomena; and its introduction into the universe of matter was necessarily the preliminary act of creation. The earth must have remained forever 'without form, and void,' and eternal darkness must have been upon the face of the deep, if the spirit of God had not first 'moved upon the face of the waters.'

" 2. Motion appears to be the simplest manifestation of power, and the idea of force seems to be primitively derived from the conscious effort which is required to produce motion. Force may, then, be regarded as having a spiritual origin, and when it is imparted to the physical world, motion **is its** usual form of mechanical exhibition.

EMANUEL SWEDENBORG

" 3. Matter is purely inert. It is susceptive of receiving and containing any amount of mechanical force which may be communicated to it, but cannot originate new force, or in any way transform the force which it has received."

VI

CONTINUED STUDY OF THE ANIMAL KINGDOM: SPIRITUAL EXPERIENCE

THUS far Swedenborg's labors have been devoted to the unfolding of the Divine revelation in the Book of Nature, by means of experiment, analysis, and the exercise of reason, under such guidance as he was prepared to receive of the Spirit of Truth. In these labors we have observed the ample training of the reasoning faculty, even to maturity, with its increasing acknowledgment of dependence on the light of the Sun of heaven. We are now to learn the preparation of heart yet necessary, in order that the submission to the guidance of the Spirit of Truth might become so entire as to direct him securely in unfolding the Divine revelation in the written Word. The groundwork of this preparation we may recognize in the Rules of Life which Sandels found, as he says in his eulogy, in more than one place among his manuscripts, and which may be commended to all of us who would fulfil the duties of this life and prepare for life in the kingdom of heaven: —

"1. Diligently to read and meditate upon the Word of God.

"2. To be content under the dispensations of God's providence.

"3. To observe a propriety of behavior, and to preserve the conscience pure.

"4. To obey what is commanded, to attend faithfully to one's office and other duties, and in addition to make one's self useful to society in general."

As marking the progress of the preparation, we find in his philosophical works, besides the growing humility and reverence that illumine the pages, some plain statements, drawn we cannot doubt from his spiritual experience. In the part of The Animal Kingdom treating of the soul, he says —

"To change the disposition is to change the very nature. To change a good disposition into an evil one is comparatively easy; but to change an evil one into a good is more difficult. This can in no way be effected except by means of the rational mind and its understanding, whether the understanding be our own, or derived from faith, or per-

SPIRITUAL EXPERIENCE

suaded by authority. Nor is the nature changed unless we become averse to evils and abhor them, and never lead our mind back into the former state; and unless whenever it slips back, we snatch it out, from the liberty given, and come into the state which agrees with the more perfect love. Not even so is it changed unless we remain a long while in this state, and meet the other with force and violence, clothing ourselves with the opposite new state by constant works and practices of virtues, and so continuing until it has become a second nature and expelled as it were the other nature — so that whenever the old nature returns, we perceive that it must be resisted. In this way and no other we can put off the evil nature and put on a good nature; but it is very difficult in this life without grace and Divine help."

These we feel to be the words of experience, of long and successful labor. But what is here described is only the reformation of the natural mind, or disposition. After this it is necessary that the natural mind should so far submit as to suffer the spiritual mind to flow in with its own loves.

"To this," Swedenborg says, "the intellect unless from what is revealed contributes nothing, but faith springing from God does the work. And so, His will being invoked, His spirit flows into the soul and changes its state, or perfects it; but the work is one of long discipline, if the soul is evil, that it may become good. . . . Hence it is plain how difficult it is to turn an evil soul into a good one, and that this is of the Divine grace alone, though there must be persevering application on the part of man."

What is here described, though in the terms of his Psychology, we cannot fail to recognize as the regeneration of water and of the spirit. The description is that of experience already, we may believe, far advanced. What was yet needed for its completion we are now to see. But we may well pause to consider how little we have ourselves accomplished, even of the reformation of the natural disposition, and how little we know in our own experience of the total regeneration sought by Swedenborg. This deep regeneration, though with his consent and coöperation, was being effected by the Lord for a purpose to Swedenborg unknown. A few years later, he wrote—

"What the acts of my life involved I could not distinguish at the time they happened, but by the

SPIRITUAL EXPERIENCE

Divine mercy of God Messiah I was afterward informed with regard to some, even many particulars. From these I was at last able to see that the Divine providence governed the acts of my life uninterruptedly from my very youth, and directed them in such a manner that by means of the knowledge of natural things I was enabled to reach a state of intelligence, and thus by the Divine mercy of God Messiah, to serve as an instrument for opening those things which are hidden interiorly in the Word of God Messiah."

Still later, Nov 11, 1766, he wrote to Oetinger —

"I was introduced by the Lord into the natural sciences, and thus prepared, and indeed from the year 1710 to 1744, when heaven was opened to me." And this he said was for the purpose —

"That the spiritual things which are being revealed at the present day may be taught and understood naturally and rationally; for spiritual truths have a correspondence with natural truths, because in these they terminate, and upon these they rest. . . . The Lord has granted me besides to love truths in a spiritual manner — that is, to love them, not for the sake of honor, nor for the sake of gain, but for the sake of the truths themselves; for he who loves truths for the sake of truth, sees them from the Lord, because the Lord is the Way and the Truth."

For a better understanding of this love of truth for the sake of truth, and of its effects, let us here read a passage or two from Swedenborg's later Heavenly Arcana: —

"Doctrine is to be drawn from the Word, and while it is being drawn man must be in enlightenment from the Lord; and he is in enlightenment when in the love of truth for the sake of truth, not for the sake of self and the world. These are they who are enlightened in the Word when they read it, and see truth, and therefrom form for themselves doctrine. The reason is, that such men communicate with heaven, thus with the Lord, and so, being enlightened from the Lord, they are led to see the truths of the Word as they are in heaven; for the Lord flows in through heaven into their understandings, the interior understanding being what is enlightened. The Lord at the same time flows in with faith, by means of the coöperation of the new will, to which it belongs to be affected with truth for the sake of truth."

SPIRITUAL EXPERIENCE

"The Lord speaks with the man of the Church in no other way than by means of the Word, for He then enlightens man so that he may see the truth; and He also gives perception so that man may perceive that it is so. But this takes place according to the quality or the desire of truth with man, and the desire of truth with man is according to the love of it. They who love truth for the sake of truth are in enlightenment, and they who love truth for the sake of good are in perception."

Of the manifestation to him of the Divine purpose, and of further steps necessary in preparation, we now learn many things from his Spiritual Diary: —

"During several years" — he notes, Aug. 27, 1748 — "not only had I dreams by which I was informed about the things on which I was writing, but I experienced also changes of state, there being a certain extraordinary light in what was written. Afterward I had many visions with closed eyes, and light was given me in an extraordinary manner. There was also an inflow from spirits, as manifest to the sense as if it had been into the senses of the body; there were infesta-

tions in various ways by evil spirits when I was in temptations; and afterward when writing anything to which the spirits had an aversion, I was almost possessed by them, so as to feel something like a tremor. Flamy lights were seen [confirming what was written] and conversations heard in the early morning, besides many other things."
" For nearly three years " — he writes in August, 1747 — " I have been allowed to perceive and notice the operation of spirits, not by a sort of internal sight, but by a sensation which is associated with a sort of obscure sight, by which I noticed their presence, which was various, their approach and departure, besides many other things."

For some years his dreams had been growing more remarkable and more significant, so that he had been led to keep a record of them. The earlier records, beginning as early as 1736, were cut from his Diary for preservation in the family and now are lost; but there is still preserved a minute account of the dreams that he had at Amsterdam and London in the spring and summer of 1744, the critical period of his spiritual experience, together with a brief memorandum of those that

SPIRITUAL EXPERIENCE

came to him in the previous December, when he had gone from Amsterdam to the Hague.

In that month he notes — "How I opposed myself to the Spirit; and how I then enjoyed this, but afterward found that it was nonsense, without life and coherence; and that consequently a great deal of what I had written, in proportion as I had rejected the power of the Spirit, was of that description; and indeed that thus all the faults are my own, but the truths are not my own. Sometimes indeed I became impatient and thought I would rebel if all did not go on with the ease I desired, after I no longer did anything for my own sake. [And again] I found my unworthiness less, and gave thanks for the grace."

This is interesting in connection with the fact that in the Economy of the Animal Kingdom, published three years before, we find some material statements which have been disproved by later researches; while in The Animal Kingdom, which he was now preparing for the press, nothing of importance is found that does not stand the test of time. It is noteworthy also that near this period he appends to some of his manuscripts the remark, "These things are true, for I have the sign" —

by which we understand him to mean the flamy sign that appeared to him as a confirmation of what was true. To others again he appends, on stating what he is going to do, "So I seem ordered." Still his struggles go on: —

"How I resisted the power of the Holy Spirit, and what took place afterward. The hideous spectres which I saw, without life — they were terrible; although bound, they kept moving in their bands. They were in company with an animal by which I and not the child was attacked. It seemed to me as if I were lying on a mountain below which was an abyss; knots were on it. I was lying there trying to hold myself up, holding on to a knot, without foothold, and an abyss underneath. This signifies that I desire to rescue myself from the abyss, which yet is not possible."

That is to say, as we understand, the abyss of natural, selfish will, out of which we are to be rescued by the Divine grace, but not possibly by our own power. In March he dreams again of the abyss, into which there is danger of falling unless he receive help.

In April, "the day before Easter, I experienced nothing the whole night, although I repeatedly

SPIRITUAL EXPERIENCE

woke up; I thought that all was past and gone, and that I had been either forsaken or exiled. About morning it seemed to me as if I were riding, and as if I had had the direction pointed out. It was however dark, and when I looked I found that I had gone astray on account of the darkness; but then it brightened up and I saw how I had gone wrong, and I noticed the way and the forests and groves which I was to go through, and also heaven behind them, and then I awoke. My thoughts then of their own accord turned upon this, and afterward on the other life, and it seemed to me as if everything was full of grace. I burst into tears at having not loved, but rather provoked, Him who had led me and pointed out the way to the kingdom of grace; and also at my being unworthy of acceptance by grace."

"Easter was on the 5th of April, when I went to the Lord's table. Temptation still continued, most in the afternoon, till six o'clock; but it assumed no definite form. It was an anxiety felt at being condemned and in hell; but in this feeling the hope given by the Holy Spirit — according to Paul's epistle to the Romans, v. 5 — remained strong. . . I was assured that my sins were forgiven, and yet I could not control my wandering thoughts so as to restrain some expressions opposed to my better judgment: I was by permission under the influence of the Evil One. The temptation was assuaged by prayer and the Word of God: faith was there in its entirety, but confidence and love seemed to be gone."

After describing a terrible conflict that followed with a snake, changing to a dog, in a dream, he adds —

"From this may be seen the nature of the temptation and, on the other hand, the greatness of God's grace by the merit of Christ and the operation of the Holy Spirit, to whom be glory forever and ever. The idea at once struck me how great the grace of the Lord is, who accounts and appropriates to us our resistance in temptation, though it is purely God's grace and is His and not our work; and He overlooks our weaknesses in it, which yet must be manifold. I thought also of the great glory our Lord dispenses after a brief period of tribulation. . . . Afterward I awoke and slept again many times and all was in answer to my thoughts, yet so that in everything there was such life and glory that I can give no description

SPIRITUAL EXPERIENCE

of it; for it was all heavenly, clear to me at the time, but afterward inexpressible. In short I was in heaven, and I heard a language which no human tongue can utter with its inherent life, nor the glory and inmost delight resulting from it. Besides, while I was awake I was in a heavenly ecstasy which is also indescribable. . . . Praise and honor and glory be to the Highest! hallowed be His Name! Holy, Holy, Lord God of Hosts!"

"By this means," he says, "I learned by experience the meaning of this, not to love the angels more than God; as they had nearly overthrown the whole work. In comparison with our Lord no attention must be paid to them, that is, to them in respect to the help they can render, since their love is far lower than His. By some rays of light in me I found that it would be the greatest happiness to become a martyr; for, on beholding inexpressible grace combined with love to God, a desire was kindled in me to undergo this torture, which is nothing compared with eternal torment; and [a sense] that the least of the things that one can offer is his life. . . . This took place in the night between Easter Sunday and Easter Monday."

EMANUEL SWEDENBORG

Here we see the inward depth of the temptation and regeneration which Swedenborg was now undergoing. All his previous efforts were external in comparison, and futile. Indeed he is learning the inefficacy and error of all merely human efforts for goodness, even those of the angels themselves. And all this was to the end that he might yield himself wholly into the Lord's hands, and become His humble, faithful servant, with a new heart and a new spirit. Nor was his personal regeneration all that was at stake. The great question as to how regeneration is accomplished was to be experimentally solved and intelligently comprehended. From the time of the Christian Fathers it had become more and more misunderstood. The Roman Catholic Church taught that it was effected by baptism and confirmed by good works. The Reformed Churches had adopted the same belief in baptism as regeneration, for those who should receive faith as the elect — denying that men can do anything about it. For the implanting of a new, true, interior Christian Church, it was essential that the real means of regeneration should be understood. Swedenborg by inheritance was a mild Lutheran. By experience he now learns that

SPIRITUAL EXPERIENCE

neither has baptism regenerated, nor his own labor in reformation; that he is in danger of the abyss from deep natural tendency to sin; that the Lord's merit cannot be imputed to him and so effect his salvation; but that to be saved he must see and confess his sinfulness, be distressed on account of it, pray to the Lord for the grace of forgiveness, making every possible effort of resistance to evil, and all with the acknowledgment that both the prayer and the effort are not his own, but given from the Lord alone. The process is, indeed, not essentially different from that we have seen already sketched in The Animal Kingdom; but it is now being accomplished in interior degrees, far beyond what Swedenborg has imagined. And in his later works he has taught us that regeneration is applicable to several distinct degrees of the mind, of which the more interior are opened and regenerated with comparatively few. And as each successive degree is nearer to the Lord, His presence and agency in its regeneration become more clearly seen; or, in other words, each successive approach to the Lord brings a new consciousness of interior tendency to sin, which must needs be deplored and submitted to Him, and a deeper consciousness that all the power of deliverance is from Him alone. All this is learning to understand and to be aided by our Lord's victory over the weakness of human nature — in fact, to see His face in the clouds of heaven.

How deeply this was impressed on Swedenborg's heart and soul we learn from his Diary: —

"This have I learned, that the only thing . . . is in all humility to thank God for His grace and to pray for it, and to recognize our own unworthiness and God's infinite grace. . . . The sum of all I found to be this, that the one thing needful is to cast one's self in all humility on our Lord's grace, to recognize one's own unworthiness, and to thank God in humility for His grace; for if there is a feeling of glorification contained in it, the tendency of which is toward our own honor — whether it is a glorification of God's grace or of anything else — such a feeling is impure. . . . I found that I was more unworthy than others and the greatest sinner for this reason, that our Lord has granted me to penetrate by thought into certain things more deeply than many others do; and the very source of sin lies in the thoughts I am carrying out, so that my sins have on that account a deeper

SPIRITUAL EXPERIENCE

foundation than those of many others: and in this I found my unworthiness and my sins greater than those of other men. For it is not sufficient to declare one's own unworthiness, since the heart may be far removed from such a declaration, and it may be a mere matter of the imagination: but actually to see that such is the case is due to the grace of the Spirit.

"Now while I was in the spirit I thought and strove by thought to attain a knowledge of how to avoid all that was impure. I noticed, however, that this intruded itself from the ground of the love of self on all occasions when anything was reflected upon; as, for instance, when any one did not regard me according to my own estimation of myself, I thought, 'O if you only knew what grace I have, you would act differently.' This then was not only impure, but originated in the love of self. At last I found this out and entreated God's forgiveness; and I then wished that others also might have the same grace, as they perhaps either have had or will have. From this I observed clearly that there was still in me that same pernicious apple which has not yet been converted, and which is Adam's root and his hereditary sin. Yes, and an infinite number of other roots of sin remain in me."

At times he trusted that his pride in his own works was subdued and would no more trouble him, but again and again he had to learn his dependence for this, as for all other grace, on the constant protection of the Lord.

"*April 10 and 11.* . . . When awake I began thinking whether all this was not mere fantasy, and I then noticed that my faith was vacillating. I therefore pressed my hands together and prayed that I might be strengthened in faith, which also took place immediately. Again when thoughts occurred to me about being worthier than others, I prayed in like manner, whereupon these thoughts at once vanished; if therefore our Lord in the least withdraw His hand from any one, he is out of the true path, and also out of faith, as has been manifestly the case with me.

"I slept this night about eleven hours and during the whole of the morning was in my usual state of internal gladness, which was nevertheless attended with a pang: this I thought arose from the power of the spirit and my own unworthiness. At last with God's help I came into these thoughts

SPIRITUAL EXPERIENCE

— that we ought to be contented with everything which pleases the Lord, because it is for the Lord to say; and further that the Spirit is not to be resisted when we receive from God the assurance that it is God's grace which does all things for our welfare; for if we are God's we must be delighted with whatever He pleases to do with His own: still we must ask the Lord for this, because not even the least thing is in our own power. For this the Lord gave me His grace. I reflected upon this, desiring to understand the reason why all this happens to me. Yet this was sinful, for my thoughts ought not to have gone in that direction, but I ought to have prayed to the Lord for power to control them. It ought to be enough for us that it so pleases the Lord. In everything we ought only to call upon Him, pray to and thank Him, and with humility recognize our own unworthiness.

"I am still weary in my body and mind; for I know nothing except my own unworthiness, and am in pain on account of being a wretched creature. I see by this knowledge that I am unworthy of the grace I have received. . . . I have therefore adopted the following motto —

EMANUEL SWEDENBORG

"God's will be done; I am Thine and not mine."

"*April 11 and 12.* . . . There is not a single thought which is not very much alloyed with uncleanness and impurity. It is therefore best that man should every hour and every moment acknowledge that he is deserving of the punishment of hell, but that God's grace and mercy which are in Jesus Christ overlook it. I have indeed observed that our whole will into which we are born, and which is ruled by the body and introduces thought, is opposed to the Spirit which does this; wherefore there is a continual strife, and we can by no manner of means unite ourselves with the Spirit, which by grace is with us; and hence it is that we are dead to everything good, but to everything evil we are inclined from ourselves. For this reason we must at all times acknowledge ourselves guilty of innumerable sins, because our Lord God knows all and we only very little about them: we know only so much as enters into our thoughts, and only when it also enters into the actions do we become convinced of it.

"*April 12 and 13.* . . . God's grace thus showed me that I had to strive after salvation

SPIRITUAL EXPERIENCE

amid fear and trembling. But I have for my motto, 'God's will be done; I am Thine and not mine;' as therefore I have given myself from myself to the Lord, He may dispose of me after His own pleasure. In the body there seemed to be something of discontent, but in the spirit joy; for the grace of our Lord does this. May God strengthen me therein!

"I was continually in a state of combat between thoughts which were antagonistic to one another. I pray Thee, O Almighty God, that Thou wouldst grant me the grace of being Thine and not mine. Pardon my saying that I am Thine and not mine; it is God's privilege and not mine to say so. I pray for the grace of being Thine, and of not being left to myself.

"*April 18 and 19.* . . . I was at Divine service, where I noticed that thoughts on matters of faith, respecting Christ, His merit, and the like, even though they be entirely favorable and confirmatory, still cause a certain disquietude, and give rise to opposing thoughts which cannot be resisted, whenever man tries to believe from his own understanding, and not from the Lord's grace. At last it was granted me by the grace of the

EMANUEL SWEDENBORG

Spirit to receive faith without reasoning upon it, and thus to be assured in respect to it. I then saw as it were below me my own thoughts by which faith was confirmed; I laughed in my mind at them, but still more at those by which they were impugned and opposed. Faith appeared to be far above the thoughts of my understanding. Then only I got peace: may God strengthen me in it! For it is His work; and mine so much the less as my thoughts, and indeed the best of them, hinder more than they are able to promote. . . . It is therefore a higher state — I am uncertain whether it is not the highest — when man by grace no longer mixes up his understanding in matters of faith; although it appears as if the Lord with some persons permits the understanding to precede such states of assurance in respect to things which concern the understanding. 'Blessed are they who believe and do not see.' This I have clearly written in the Prologue [to The Animal Kingdom]; yet of my own self I could never have discovered this or arrived at the knowledge of it, but God's grace has wrought this, I being unconscious of it: afterward, however, I perceived it from the very effect and the change in my whole

SPIRITUAL EXPERIENCE

interior being. This therefore is God's grace and His work, and to Him alone belongs eternal glory. From this I see how difficult it is for the learned, more indeed than for the unlearned, to arrive at such a faith, and consequently to conquer themselves so as to be able to smile at themselves; for man's worship of his own understanding must first of all be abolished and overthrown, and this is God's work and not man's. It is also God's work for man to continue him in that state. Faith is in this way separated from our understanding and resides above it. This is pure faith; the other, so long as it is mixed up with our own understanding, is impure. Man's understanding must be put in bonds, and under the government of faith. The ground of faith however must be this, that He who has spoken it is God over all and Truth itself. That we must become like little children is to be understood, it seems, in this sense. . . . Faith then is purely God's gift, and is received by man when he lives according to the commandments of God and continually prays to God for it."

Such experience and testimony is most valuable on the part of him who was at the very time engaged in exploring the philosophy of the soul in the body, to the end that the way might be made clearer for the understanding to arrive at the true objects of faith. It is to be noted, however, that the submission of the understanding which he here enjoins, is to the faith given by the grace of God in the inner mind.

"*April 21 and 22.* . . . **O**n awaking I heard the words, 'All is grace;' by which is meant that all that has happened is of grace and for the best. Afterward, because it seemed to me I was so far separated from God that I could not yet think of Him in a sufficiently vivid manner, I came into a state of doubt whether I should not direct my journey homeward; a crowd of confused reasons came and my body was seized with a tremor. Yet I gathered courage and perceived that I had come here to do what was best of all, and that I had received a talent for the promotion of God's glory. I saw that all had helped together to this end; that the Spirit had been with me from my youth for this very purpose; wherefore I considered myself unworthy of life unless I followed the straight course. I then smiled at the other seducing thoughts, and thus at luxury, riches, and dis-

SPIRITUAL EXPERIENCE

tinction which I had pursued. All these I saw to be vain; and I discovered that he who is without them and is contented, is happier than he who possesses them. I therefore smiled at all arguments by which I might be confirmed, and with God's help made a resolution. May God grant His help! . . . I further noticed that faith is a sure confidence which is received from God, which nevertheless consists in every man's acting according to his talent for doing good to his neighbor, and continually more and more; that a man must do so from faith, because God has so ordered it, and must not reason any more about it, but do the work of love from obedience to faith, even though this be opposed to the lusts of the body and its persuasions. Wherefore faith without works is not the right kind of faith. A man must in reality forsake himself."

Thus we find Swedenborg learning by experience, from his own needs and under Divine guidance, what saving faith is. From another dream he learns "that God speaks with me, and that I comprehend only the least portion of what He says, because it is in representations, of which I understand as yet but very little; and further that He hears and perceives everything that is spoken and every thought that any one entertains."

From other representative dreams he understands "that I must employ my remaining time in writing upon that which is higher, and not upon worldly things which are far below; and indeed that I must write about that which concerns the very centre of all, and that which concerns Christ. May God be so gracious as to enlighten me respecting my duty, for I am still in some obscurity as to the direction whither I am to turn."

Early in May, 1744, he went to London for the better prosecution of his work on The Animal Kingdom. His dreams, interior struggles, and thorough purification were continued.

"*May 5 and 6.* . . . This now is the sum of all: First, that there is nothing but grace by which we can be saved. Second, grace is in Jesus Christ, who is the seat of grace. Third, love to God in Christ promotes salvation. Fourth, man then allows himself to be led by the spirit of Jesus. Fifth, everything that comes from ourselves is dead, and is nothing but sin, and worthy

SPIRITUAL EXPERIENCE

of eternal damnation. Sixth, for good can come from no other source than from the Lord."

Still laboring in the day-time on The Animal Kingdom, a large share of his dreams at night relate to his studies; sometimes encouraging him to expect in them the Divine assistance, sometimes warning him not to be withdrawn by them too far from what was more holy and of more importance. In this work, which he had undertaken of his own counsel, we cannot suppose that he would be easily freed from confidence in his own abilities.

August 5 he notes, "I boasted [in a dream] of my strength, in the presence of Assessor B. This signifies that daily I sin against my God in the thoughts which cling to me, and from which no man, but God alone, can deliver me; likewise that I had boasted to D. H. about my work. On the following day I had intended to go to the communion; but I forbore when from the above I found that none but God alone can give absolution from sins; wherefore it was given me also to observe some things with respect to confession."

Here we may take leave of Swedenborg's scien-

EMANUEL SWEDENBORG

tific pursuits, remarking only that their results are in train soon to receive greater attention than ever before, in consequence of being newly published in sumptuous style and great completeness by the Royal Swedish Academy of Sciences.

VII

OPENING OF SPIRITUAL SIGHT: UNFOLDING OF THE WORD

ABOUT this time Swedenborg began to project his treatise on the Worship and Love of God. He seems to have felt a Divine call to write it, and at times to have doubted whether he ought not to leave his other work for the purpose. Yet, it was with reference to this treatise that he received the following caution:—

"*October 6 and 7.* . . . Afterward I lighted upon these thoughts and received this instruction, namely, that all love for whatever object — as, for instance, for the work on which I am now engaged — when the object is loved in itself and not as a means to the only love, which is to God and Jesus Christ, is a meretricious love. For this reason also this love is always compared in the Word of God to whoredom. This I have also experienced in myself. But when love to God is man's chief love, then he does not entertain for these objects any other kind of love than that of promoting thereby his love of God."

As thoughts on religion filled his mind he became full of zeal to instruct others. "Afterward I seemed to say to myself that the Lord Himself will instruct me. For, as I discovered, I am in such a state that I know nothing on this subject except that Christ must be all in all, or God through Christ, so that we of ourselves cannot contribute the least toward it, and still less strive for it: wherefore it is best to surrender at discretion, and were it possible to be altogether passive in this matter, it would be a state of perfection. I saw also in a vision how some beautiful bread was presented to me on a plate. This was a prediction that the Lord Himself will instruct me, as soon as I have attained that state in which I shall know nothing, and in which all my preconceived notions will be removed from me; which is the first state of learning: or in other words that I must first become a child, and that then I shall be able to be nurtured in knowledge, as is being done with me now."

On the 27th of October he began the work on the Worship and Love of God, and laid aside,

OPENING OF SPIRITUAL SIGHT

never to resume, The Animal Kingdom. "May God lead me in the right way! Christ said that I must not undertake anything without Him."

"In the morning on awaking I fell into a swoon or fainting fit, similar to that which I experienced about six or seven years ago at Amsterdam, when I entered upon the Economy of the Animal Kingdom; but it was much more subtile, so that I was almost dead. It came upon me as soon as I saw the light. I threw myself upon my face, when it gradually passed off. In the mean time short, interrupted slumbers took possession of me; so that this swoon or *deliquium* was deeper, but I soon got over it. This signifies that my head is being cleared, and is in fact being cleansed of all that would obstruct these thoughts — as was also the case the last time, because it gave me penetration, especially whilst writing. This was represented to me now in that I appeared to write a fine hand."

Coincidently with his increasing submission of heart to the Divine guidance, we find a growing sensitiveness or openness to spiritual impressions. Indeed, whether as a constitutional peculiarity or from depth of thought, Swedenborg had a certain faculty of retrocession from physical activity when thinking deeply. In The Animal Kingdom he had remarked, "When the mind is thinking very intently and breathing tacitly and slowly, then the lungs elevated to a certain degree appear in like manner to keep silence, and to send out and draw in the air almost imperceptibly, so as not to disturb the analyses of the rational mind by any motion on their part." And again, "If we carefully attend to profound thoughts, we shall find that when we draw breath, a host of ideas rush from beneath as through an open door into the sphere of thought, whereas when we hold the breath, and slowly let it out, we deeply keep the while in the tenor of our thought, and communicate as it were with the higher faculty of the soul — as I have observed in my own person times without number. Retaining or holding back the breath is equivalent to having intercourse with the soul: attracting or drawing it in amounts to intercourse with the body."

But it was long after spiritual manifestations began to occur to him before he thought of the possibility of conversing with spirits. Indeed, he knew nothing about spirits. He believed in the

OPENING OF SPIRITUAL SIGHT

Holy Spirit and in the power of the devil. He believed in angels, but knew nothing of the world filled with the spirits and angels who had once been men. We see how gradually the knowledge came to him:—

"*October 3 to 6.* I have noticed several times that there are various kinds of spirits. The One Spirit, which is that of Christ, is the only one that has all blessedness with it; by other spirits man is enticed a thousand ways to follow them, but woe to those who do so. Another time Korah and Dathan occurred to me, who brought strange fire to the altar and could not offer it. Such is the case when a different fire is introduced than that which comes from Christ. I saw also something like a fire coming to me. It is necessary therefore that a distinction should be made between spirits, which however cannot be done except through Christ Himself and His Spirit."

Some years later, after referring to the sundry spiritual manifestations which we have already described, he says —

"At last a spirit spoke a few words to me, when I was greatly astonished at his perceiving my thoughts. Afterward, when my mind was opened, I was greatly astonished that I could converse with spirits; as the spirits were astonished that I should wonder. From this it may be concluded how difficult it is for man to believe that he is governed by the Lord through spirits, and how difficult it is for him to give up the opinion that he lives his own life of himself without the agency of spirits."

The date of this occurrence appears to have been the middle of April, 1745, while still engaged perhaps on The Worship and Love of God. The fullest account preserved is given by his friend Robsahm, who says that in answer to his own inquiry where and how it was granted him to see and hear what takes place in the other world, Swedenborg answered —

"I was in London, and dined rather late at the inn where I was in the habit of dining and where I had my own room. My thoughts were engaged on the subjects we have been discussing. I was hungry and ate with a good appetite. Toward the close of the meal I noticed a sort of dimness before my eyes; this became denser, and I then saw the floor covered with the most horrid crawling reptiles, such as snakes, frogs, and similar crea-

OPENING OF SPIRITUAL SIGHT

tures. I was amazed, for I was perfectly conscious and my thoughts were clear. At last the darkness increased still more; but it disappeared all at once, and I then saw a man sitting in the corner of the room: as I was then alone I was very much frightened at his words; for he said, '*Eat not so much.*' All became black again before my eyes, but immediately it cleared away and I found myself alone in the room."

That this "man" was a spirit appears from Swedenborg's statement about his astonishment when a spirit first spoke a few words to him, and from Robsahm's own statement that this account was given in answer to his inquiry where and how he first came to see and hear spirits. It would seem then that Robsahm has made a little confusion in what he goes on to say about *the same man's* appearing the following night. And yet as, according to Swedenborg, when the Lord appears to angels and men, He does so by filling an angel with His presence and speaking through his mouth, it may be that it was the same angel from the Lord who had been present with him in the spiritual thoughts on which he was engaged in the day-time, and then warned him not to yield too much to the demands of the body, and again in the night instructed him as to the labors for which the Lord was preparing him — first seeming as a man, giving human admonition, and then as the Lord, uttering His commands. According to Robsahm, Swedenborg continued — " I went home, and during the night the same man revealed himself to me again, but I was not frightened now. He then said that he was the Lord God, the Creator of the world, and the Redeemer, and that He had chosen me to unfold to men the spiritual sense of the Scripture, and that He Himself would show to me what I should write on this subject. That same night also were opened to me, so that I became thoroughly convinced of their reality, the world of spirits, heaven, and hell; and I recognized there many acquaintances of every condition in life. From that day I gave up the study of all worldly science and labored in spiritual things, according as the Lord had commanded me to write. Afterward the Lord opened my eyes, very often daily, so that in midday I could see into the other world, and in a state of perfect wakefulness converse with angels and spirits."

OPENING OF SPIRITUAL SIGHT

The remarkable absence of dignity and circumstance, such as imagination would invent, in this first introduction to the sight and hearing of the other world, witnesses nothing against its plain truth. We may wonder that the first announcement should be so simple a prohibition. On this Swedenborg says not a word. We have no reason to suppose him an inordinate eater; but doubtless in hunger he gave himself up for the time to the body's demand for satisfaction, and his mind fell from its high thoughts. The spirits or angels with him would perceive his fall and would, if opportunity were given, rebuke him. Fasting as well as prayer is the means of release from selfishness and evil. With Swedenborg there had been reformation of life, and then internal regeneration of a very deep kind. This regeneration must needs work outward till it cleansed the whole life, more perfectly, because from internal ground, than the first reformation could do. It may well be that the last stronghold of selfish spirits, not yet given up to the Lord of all, was that of outward sense. So our Lord Himself finished the work of purifying His humanity by overcoming the resistance of the body. So the last thing He did for the disciples, before giving to them the bread and the wine that represented His own life, was to wash their feet, that they might be clean every whit. So too, Swedenborg tells us, those who are internally prepared for heaven and who have been delivered from all evil except that which belongs to the infirmities of the body, are taken up into heaven immediately after death. That from this time forth he himself enjoyed a remarkable protection from spirits who would have excited vain thoughts about his own works and the grace vouchsafed him, is manifest in everything he wrote, if we except a certain floridity of style in this work already in hand on the Worship and Love of God, in which he himself later detected " somewhat of egotism." Dr. Wilkinson well says of the change that now came over him —

" Certainly, in turning from his foregone life to that which now occupies us, we seem to be treating of another person — of one on whom the great change has passed, who has tasted the blessings of death and disburdened his spiritual part, of mundane cares, sciences, and philosophies. The spring of his lofty flights in nature sleeps in

OPENING OF SPIRITUAL SIGHT

the dust beneath his feet. The liberal charm of his rhetoric is put off, never to be resumed. . . . It is a clear instance of disembodiment — of emancipation from a worldly lifetime; and we have now to contemplate Swedenborg, still a mortal, as he rose into the other world. From that elevation he as little recurred to his scientific life, though he had its spirit with him, as a freed soul to the body in the tomb: he only possessed it in a certain high memory, which offered its result to his new pursuits."

All his mental labors had served as efficient training for the work now laid out for him. But what he had begun to find even in philosophic study — the need to lay down all thought of himself — became imperative, the *sine qua non* for submitting wholly to the guidance of the Holy Spirit in unfolding the true inner meaning of the Scriptures. He never forgot that the Lord alone could unloose the seals of the Book, and reveal Himself therein. He had already gained the truth that the material things of the body correspond in their use to the spiritual things of the soul, and that herein was the key to the true understanding of the Scriptures. But what

EMANUEL SWEDENBORG

did he know of the spiritual things of the soul? of the things of heaven, and of the Divine providence therein? In all this he was to be instructed by the Lord Himself in His Word, but with the aid of open communication with angels and spirits whose life this inner meaning is.

It is now the year 1745. The time is ripening for the judgment. The clouds obscuring the face of the Son of Man are at their darkest. It is time for the dawn of the light that is to come. The light of the Lord's presence is to begin to be seen in His written Word. The age of miracles compelling belief is past. Man is to be instructed in an orderly, rational manner. One mind has been prepared and taught its mission. Through its labors the light is to have a point of diffusion on earth, and still more by ready communication in the spirit world among the multitudes there gathered who clung to their erroneous interpretations of Scripture, from which they could not be released until the unsealing of the Book by the Lamb. That this unsealing should be, not an instantaneous, but a gradual process, and that it should have effect in the world where the letter of the Book belongs, is in keeping with

OPENING OF SPIRITUAL SIGHT

the orderly, gradual course of the Divine providence. Twelve years were devoted by Swedenborg to writing and publishing what was revealed to him in the Scriptures, before the judgment in the world of spirits was seen by him to come to its fulfilment.

Though assured of the Divine sanction and aid in the office intrusted to him, Swedenborg entered upon the task in natural and scientific manner. He procured the best editions of the Scriptures in the original languages, studied them diligently from beginning to end time after time, and then began making short notes — *Adversaria* — much as do ordinary commentators, together with several Biblical indexes for future use. All this was preliminary study, not for print, occupying nearly two years. In 1747 he was ready for the service required of him and prepared for the press the first volume of his *Arcana Cœlestia*, in which he unfolds verse by verse the internal content of the first fifteen chapters of Genesis. This was the beginning of the fulfilment of his mission, the nature of which is set forth in the introduction to the volume: —

"I. That the Word of the Old Testament contains arcana of heaven, and that all and each of the things therein regard the Lord, His heaven, the Church, faith, and the things which are of faith, no mortal apprehends from the letter; for from the letter or the sense of the letter no one sees anything else than that they regard in general the external things of the Jewish Church; when yet there are everywhere internal things which are nowhere manifest in the external, except a very few which the Lord revealed and explained to the Apostles; as, that sacrifices signify the Lord, that the land of Canaan and Jerusalem signify heaven, whence Canaan and Jerusalem are called heavenly and Paradise.

"II. But that all things and each, yea the most particular, even to the least jot, signify and involve spiritual and heavenly things, the Christian world is hitherto profoundly ignorant, and so it has little regard for the Old Testament. Yet the truth might be known merely from this, that the Word, because it is the Lord's and from the Lord, could in no wise be given without containing interiorly such things as are of heaven, of the Church, and of faith; not otherwise could it be called the Word of the Lord, nor could it be

OPENING OF SPIRITUAL SIGHT

said that there is any life in it; for whence is its life unless from those things which are of life? that is, unless from this, that all and each of the things in it have reference to the Lord, who is the very Life itself? Wherefore whatsoever does not interiorly regard Him, does not live; nay, whatever expression in the Word does not involve Him, or in its own manner relate to Him, is not Divine.

"III. Without such life the Word as to the letter is dead; for it is with the Word as with man, who, as is known in the Christian world, is external and internal; the external man separate from the internal is the body, and thus dead; but the internal is what lives and gives to the external to live. The internal man is the soul. Thus the Word as to the letter alone is as the body without the soul.

"IV. From the sense of the letter alone, when the mind is fixed in it, can in no wise be seen that it contains such things; as in this first part of Genesis, from the sense of the letter nothing else is known than that it treats of the creation of the world and of the Garden of Eden, which is called Paradise; also of Adam as the first created man: who imagines anything more? But that these things contain arcana which have never hitherto been revealed, will be sufficiently evident from what follows; and indeed that the first chapter of Genesis in the internal sense treats of the NEW CREATION of man, or of his REGENERATION, in general, and of the Most Ancient Church in particular; and indeed in such manner that there is not the least particle of an expression that does not represent, signify, and involve these things.

"V. But that such is the case no mortal can ever know unless from the Lord. For this reason it is permitted to state at the outset that of the Lord's mercy it has been granted me now for several years to be constantly and continuously in the company of spirits and angels, to hear them speaking and in turn to speak with them; hence it has been given me to hear and see astonishing things which are in the other life, which have never come to the knowledge of any man, nor into his idea. I have there been instructed concerning different kinds of spirits, concerning the state of souls after death, concerning hell or the lamentable state of the unfaithful, concerning heaven

OPENING OF SPIRITUAL SIGHT

or the most happy state of the faithful, especially concerning the doctrine of faith which is acknowledged in the whole heaven; on which subjects by the Divine mercy of the Lord many things will be said in the following pages."

Following this introduction is printed the whole of the first chapter of Genesis in Latin. Then is given a summary of the contents of the chapter in the internal sense:—

"The six days, or times, which are so many successive states of man's regeneration, are in general as follows:—

"The first state is that which precedes, both from infancy and immediately before regeneration, and is called a void, emptiness, and thick darkness. And the first movement, which is the mercy of the Lord, is the spirit of God moving itself upon the faces of the waters.

"The second state is when distinction is made between the things which are the Lord's and those which are man's own; those which are the Lord's are called in the Word 'remains,' and are here especially the knowledges of faith which man has acquired from infancy, which are stored up and are not manifest before he comes into this state. This state seldom exists at the present day without temptation, misfortune, or grief, which cause the things of the body and the world, or his own, to become quiet and as it were die. Thus the things of the external man are separated from those of the internal: in the internal are the remains stored up by the Lord for this time and this use.

"The third state is that of repentance, in which from the internal man he speaks piously and devoutly, and brings forth good things, as the works of charity, but which are nevertheless inanimate because he regards them as from himself. These are called the tender grass, then the herb yielding seed, and afterward the tree yielding fruit.

"The fourth state is when he is affected by love and illumined by faith; he before indeed spoke pious things and brought forth good things, but from a state of temptation and distress, not from faith and charity. These therefore, love and faith, are now enkindled in the internal man, and are called the two great lights.

"The fifth state is, that he speaks from faith and thereby confirms himself in truth and good; the things which he then brings forth are ani-

OPENING OF SPIRITUAL SIGHT

mate, and are called the fishes of the sea and the birds of the heavens.

"The sixth state is when from faith and thence from love he speaks true things and does good things; the things which he then brings forth are called the living soul and creature. And because he then begins to act from love also, as well as from faith, he becomes a spiritual man, which is called an image of God. His spiritual life is delighted and sustained by the things that are of the knowledges of faith and of the works of charity, which are called his food; and his natural life is delighted and sustained by the things that are of the body and the senses; from which there is a combat until love reigns and he becomes a celestial man.

"They who are regenerated do not all arrive at this state, but some, and the greatest part at this day, only to the first; some only to the second; some to the third, the fourth, and the fifth; few to the sixth, and scarce any to the seventh."

The seventh state, here but alluded to, is described in the next chapter, in the explanation of the seventh day. After this summary of the contents of the first chapter, he begins with the particular unfolding of the internal sense, verse by verse, clause by clause, premising that —

"In the following pages by the LORD is meant solely the Saviour of the world, Jesus Christ; and He is called Lord without the other names. He is acknowledged and adored as Lord in the entire heaven, because He has all power in the heavens and in the earth. He commanded also saying, 'Ye call Me Lord, and ye say rightly, for I am' (John xiii. 13). And after the resurrection the disciples called Him Lord.

"Through the whole heaven they know no other Father than the Lord, because they are One, as He said: 'I am the way, the truth, and the life.' Philip saith, 'Show us the Father.' Jesus saith to him, 'Am I so long time with you, and yet hast thou not known Me, Philip? He that hath seen Me hath seen the Father: how sayest thou then, show us the Father? Believest thou not that I am in the Father and the Father in Me? Believe Me that I am in the Father and the Father in Me' (John xiv. 6-11)."

Twenty-six octavo pages are given to the explication of this first chapter, and then it is said —

"This then is the internal sense of the Word,

OPENING OF SPIRITUAL SIGHT

its very life, which does not at all appear from the sense of the letter; but the arcana are so many that volumes would not be sufficient for unfolding them. Here only a few are declared, and such as may prove that regeneration is here treated of, and that this proceeds from the external man to the internal. Thus the angels understand the Word. They know nothing at all which is of the letter, not even one word of what it proximately signifies, still less the names of countries, cities, rivers, and persons, which occur so frequently in the historic and prophetic parts. They have only an idea of the things signified by words and names; as, by Adam in Paradise they have a perception of the Most Ancient Church, and not of the Church itself, but of the faith toward the Lord of that Church; by Noah, the Church remaining with posterity and continued to the time of Abram; by Abraham, not the man who lived, but the saving faith which he represented; and so on. Thus they perceive things spiritual and celestial, altogether abstracted from words and names."

An appropriate beginning is this of the work to which Swedenborg was to devote the remaining

EMANUEL SWEDENBORG

thirty years of his life — that of causing the face of the Son of Man to be seen in the clouds of the letter of His Word. To this task he brought certain important qualifications: —

First, inherited reverence for the Scriptures, as the Word of God. Second, intimacy therewith by daily reading and meditation. Third, conviction through philosophic study that all material things are the representatives or correspondents of spiritual things, and that this correspondence is the key to the understanding of Holy Scripture. Fourth, knowledge by experience that truth must be sought for its own sake, with no thought of merit or personal advantage. Fifth, certainty that he was Divinely called to this service and would be Divinely protected and guided in it. Sixth, experience of the enlightenment given to the self-denying seeker of truth for the truth's sake. Seventh, living consciousness of the presence of the Lord in the inner sense of His Word — as described in his last published work: — "To the end that the Lord might be continually present, He has disclosed to me the spiritual sense of His Word, in which Divine truth is in its light, and in this light He is constantly present."

OPENING OF SPIRITUAL SIGHT

To all this was added the ineffable grace of being able to see and converse with the angels of heaven, who perceive in the Scriptures all the inner meaning applicable to their own capacity and needs. Nevertheless in his unfolding of the Word for the use of men he was not, he says, permitted to take anything from any angel, but solely from the Word itself under the guidance of the Holy Spirit. With all this guidance and never without, Swedenborg used scientific method in his studies, everything he wrote having passed through the alembic of his rational thought, to the end that it might be accepted by the rational thought of men. Thus throughout his explications of the Word he is continually drawing and demonstrating the internal meaning by citation of divers other passages in which the expression in question has the meaning he now assigns to it. This was the purpose of his indexes. And further, as he goes on, he continually refers back to previous numbers in which the same subject has been treated. By these constant citations and references it is that his volumes of explications become so bulky, the Arcana unfolded in Genesis and Exodus making in English twenty volumes.

thirty years of his life — that of causing the face of the Son of Man to be seen in the clouds of the letter of His Word. To this task he brought certain important qualifications: —

First, inherited reverence for the Scriptures, as the Word of God. Second, intimacy therewith by daily reading and meditation. Third, conviction through philosophic study that all material things are the representatives or correspondents of spiritual things, and that this correspondence is the key to the understanding of Holy Scripture. Fourth, knowledge by experience that truth must be sought for its own sake, with no thought of merit or personal advantage. Fifth, certainty that he was Divinely called to this service and would be Divinely protected and guided in it. Sixth, experience of the enlightenment given to the self-denying seeker of truth for the truth's sake. Seventh, living consciousness of the presence of the Lord in the inner sense of His Word — as described in his last published work: — "To the end that the Lord might be continually present, He has disclosed to me the spiritual sense of His Word, in which Divine truth is in its light, and in this light He is constantly present."

OPENING OF SPIRITUAL SIGHT

To all this was added the ineffable grace of being able to see and converse with the angels of heaven, who perceive in the Scriptures all the inner meaning applicable to their own capacity and needs. Nevertheless in his unfolding of the Word for the use of men he was not, he says, permitted to take anything from any angel, but solely from the Word itself under the guidance of the Holy Spirit. With all this guidance and never without, Swedenborg used scientific method in his studies, everything he wrote having passed through the alembic of his rational thought, to the end that it might be accepted by the rational thought of men. Thus throughout his explications of the Word he is continually drawing and demonstrating the internal meaning by citation of divers other passages in which the expression in question has the meaning he now assigns to it. This was the purpose of his indexes. And further, as he goes on, he continually refers back to previous numbers in which the same subject has been treated. By these constant citations and references it is that his volumes of explications become so bulky, the Arcana unfolded in Genesis and Exodus making in English twenty volumes.

EMANUEL SWEDENBORG

Interspersed, however, with the chapters, are short treatises on many kindred subjects, some doctrinal and others descriptive of the other world.

The original Latin edition of the Arcana was completed in 1758 in eight large quarto volumes, published in London. During this period of eleven years nothing else was published by the author, and little else written save many volumes of notes of his spiritual experience. These have since been published by his friends both in Latin and in English, under the title of his Spiritual Diary, and the most important of their contents are to be found here and there as needed in his own publications.

VIII

"THE APOCALYPSE EXPLAINED" AND OTHER WORKS

IN the Arcana of the Books of Moses, and collaterally in the other Books of the Old Testament, Swedenborg had found a constant foreshadowing of the eventual coming of the Lord to dwell with men their God. In other terms, he had seen the inner Word to be the revelation of the Divine purpose toward mankind, inducing always the Divine image and likeness, and in due time to be fully accomplished by this purpose, or the Word, becoming flesh and dwelling among men. This great event in the history of mankind we are wont to regard as wholly completed in the Gospel period, while our Lord remained visible in the flesh. But this was only the beginning, the introduction to the Lord's dwelling with men in their souls, their hearts, and even in their flesh. By coming down, or coming forth from within, into all the degrees of human life, even to the flesh, in the single form taken from woman, the Divine

EMANUEL SWEDENBORG

Purpose, the Word, the Divine Will toward men, entered into human clothing and became forever present and operative with man, as he will accept it for his own — not indeed in continued visible presence, which could be but in one spot and there compelling, but throughout the world for all time in the record of the Gospel and within the heart as the Holy Spirit to those that love His commandments and do them.

This inner presence became real to the disciples after the outward presence left them, and inspired them to preach and heal in His name. But it was less and less realized in succeeding generations till — even as the Lord had foretold — all perception of it was lost. In fact, the understanding of it by the first disciples was not what would have been given if they could have received it. They thought of their Lord as they had seen Him — as a Divine Person, the Only-begotten Son, in the bosom and at the right hand of the Father. It was with this idea that Judas wondered how He could manifest Himself to them and not to the world. And we may doubt whether any understood the Lord's answer — "If a man love Me, he will keep My word; and My Father will love

THE APOCALYPSE EXPLAINED

him, and We will come unto him and make Our abode with him." For all the pains their Lord had taken to make them understand that He was but the manifestation of the Father's will in their human degree of life, they could not realize that when He had laid down the human form taken from the mother Mary, He would thereafter be with them and all who would love Him — not in limited bodily form, but as the Father's will in the Divinely human form of thought and feeling, which is the Word in essence and which He had revealed to them in the flesh.

This Divine Human presence manifesting itself by the Holy Spirit, calling all things to our remembrance whatsoever He has said unto us in all the Scriptures, the Church has been slow to apprehend. Only in love can it be apprehended. An age must pass of faulty apprehension in which the love of the many will wax cold. But John should endure to the end. There should yet be gleanings of the olive, a few berries in the topmost boughs of the Church, some of the love represented by John, when the time should be fulfilled for the new recognition of their Lord in His Word.

EMANUEL SWEDENBORG

John in vision saw the Son of Man in the midst of seven golden candlesticks, with all heavenly light and love. The golden candlesticks, according to Swedenborg, represent the acceptance in the heavens of this the Lord's light in His Divine Human manifestation. John's falling at His feet as dead represents the utter abasement of all merely human conceit when this Divine presence is apprehended in the Word. John as representing the loving acceptance of the Divine Human presence represents also the teaching of this presence, and thus his addresses to the churches represent the effect of this teaching, or doctrine, on the various states of those of the Church who are in the end to compose it in its new age — that of the New Jerusalem. In the fifth chapter of his vision the opening of the Book by the Lamb describes the effect of its interior light on the interiors of men in both worlds. Thus the Book is at once the book of the Word and the book of men's lives as it searches and judges them. And the remaining chapters are filled with the particulars of this judgment, condemning and consigning to their homes those whose hearts and lives are opposed to the Divine will, enlightening and enrol-

THE APOCALYPSE EXPLAINED

ling in a new Christian heaven those whose hearts are open to this will.

All the while that this true understanding of the Divine Human presence was descending from heaven into the world of spirits and executing the judgment there, Swedenborg was on earth recording both the judgment and the interior significance of the vision to John, in his "Apocalypse Explained." The judgment he describes as being effected during the year 1757. In that year and the one or two following he was preparing this work for the press in four large volumes. At first the method pursued is that of the Arcana, giving the high internal explication of each verse and word, with abounding citations from other parts of the Word in confirmation, with their internal meaning. And as in the Arcana, though true doctrine is drawn from the Word in contrast with the false doctrine condemned, but little is said of the new church by which the true is to be held, and that little speaks of it as probably, like the first Christian, to be established among the Gentiles. When however he comes to the fourteenth chapter, he finds the woman encompassed with the sun and with the moon at her feet, to represent the love for the Lord remaining in the Church, which was to bring forth the true doctrine — the man-child — and to become the new stage of the Church.

This becomes more and more apparent to him as he advances in the explication, and as he finds at the conclusion of the judgment a new heaven being formed of those from the Christian world who had in patience been awaiting the new light and now found their place in this heaven of the new church to be founded on earth. With this new understanding of the coming age of the Christian Church, as he came nearer its more particular description, he stayed his hand in the nineteenth chapter and laid this nearly completed work aside, not to be printed until by his friends after his death. Instead he now first published several smaller treatises, on "The Final Judgment," on "Heaven and Hell," "The Earths in the Universe," and "The New Jerusalem and its Heavenly Doctrine." Then he took up the Apocalypse anew and in 1766 produced a much smaller work entitled "The Apocalypse Revealed," omitting in great part the numerous citations from other parts of Scripture which, with their explication,

THE APOCALYPSE EXPLAINED

made the former work so voluminous. And from the very beginning of this later work he treats of those of the Christian Church of the first age who on being enlightened are to form the Church in its new age — the New Church of the New Jerusalem, the genuine Christian Church. The descent of the light of the Divine Human presence through heaven effecting the judgment in the world of spirits and for a beginning on this earth, was already bringing this enlightenment and was forming the new heaven.

The part taken in this judgment and enlightenment by Swedenborg's reception of this new light from the inner sense of the Word, with its publication and demonstration from the Word in the letter, is not set forth by him, but may in some degree be inferred. We have seen the doctrine of salvation by faith alone attacked by him from boyhood. It was the dominant power in the Protestant Church of his day, and his attacks which pervaded his theological works aroused the hostility of the Swedish clergy in this world, as well as of the numberless supporters of this doctrine in the world of spirits. Of the virulence with which his demonstration of the falsity of this doctrine was attacked, and of the effects in the world of spirits of this demonstration from the Scriptures, a striking example is related by him at the close of his explication of the eleventh chapter of the Apocalypse : —

" I was once seized suddenly with a disease that seemed to threaten my life. I suffered excruciating pain all over my head; a pestilent smoke ascended from that Jerusalem [in the world of spirits] which is called Sodom and Egypt; half dead with the severity of my sufferings, I expected every moment would be my last. Thus I lay in my bed three days and a half; my spirit was reduced to this state, and my body in consequence. And then I heard the voices of persons about me, saying, 'Lo, he who preached repentance for the remission of sins, and the man Christ alone, lies dead in the streets of our city.' And they asked some of the clergy whether he was worthy of burial; who answered, 'No, let him lie to be gazed at.' And they passed to and fro, and mocked. All this befell me, of a truth, when I was writing the explanation of this chapter of the Apocalypse. Then were heard many shocking speeches of scoffers who said, 'How can repentance be performed

THE APOCALYPSE EXPLAINED

without faith? And how can the man Christ be adored as God? Since we are saved of free grace without any merit of our own, what need is there of any faith but this — that God the Father sent the Son to take away the curse of the law, to impute his merit to us, and so to justify us in His sight, and absolve us from our sins by the declaration of a priest, and then give the Holy Ghost to operate all good in us? Are not these doctrines agreeable to Scripture, and consistent with reason also?' All this the crowd who stood by agreed to and applauded. I heard what passed without the power of replying, being almost dead; but after three days and a half my spirit recovered, and being in the spirit I left the street and went into the city, and said again, 'Do the work of repentance and believe in Christ, and your sins will be remitted and ye will be saved; but otherwise ye will perish. Did not the Lord Himself preach repentance for the remission of sins, and that men should believe in Him? Did not He enjoin His disciples to preach the same? Is not a full and fatal security of life the sure consequence of this dogma of your faith?' But they replied, 'What idle talk! Has not the Son made satisfaction?

EMANUEL SWEDENBORG

And does not the Father impute it to us, and justify us who have believed in it? Thus are we led by the spirit of grace; how then can sin have place in us, and what power has death over us? Do you comprehend this Gospel, thou preacher of sin and repentance?' At that instant a voice was heard from heaven, saying, 'What is the faith of an impenitent man but a dead faith? The end is come, the end is come upon you that are secure, blameless in your own eyes, justified in your own faith, ye devils.' And suddenly a deep gulf was opened in the midst of the city, which spread itself far and wide, and the houses fell one upon another and were swallowed up; and presently water began to bubble up from the wide whirlpool, and overflowed the waste.

"When they were thus overwhelmed and, to appearance, drowned, I was desirous to know their condition in the deep; and a voice from heaven said to me, 'Thou shalt see and hear.' And straightway the waters in which they seemed to be drowned, disappeared; for waters in the spiritual world are correspondences, and hence appear to surround those who are in falsities. Then they appeared to me in a sandy place, where there **were**

THE APOCALYPSE EXPLAINED

large heaps of stones, amongst which they were running, and lamenting that they were cast out of their great city; and they lifted up their voices and cried, 'Why has all this befallen us? Are we not by our faith clean, pure, just, and holy? . . . Have we not made reconciliation, propitiation, expiation, and are thus absolved, washed, and cleansed from sins? And is not the curse of the law taken away by Christ? Why then are we cast down here as the damned? We have been told by a presumptuous preacher of sin in our great city, "Believe in Christ and repent." But have we not believed in Christ while we believed in His merit? And have we not done the work of repentance while we confessed ourselves sinners? Why then has all this befallen us?' But immediately a voice from one side said to them, 'Do you know any one sin that is in you? Have you ever examined yourselves? Have you in consequence shunned any evil as a sin against God? For he who does not shun sin, remains in it; and is not sin the Devil? Ye are therefore of the class of whom the Lord said, Then shall ye begin to say, "We have eaten and drunk in Thy presence, and Thou hast taught in our streets;" but He shall say, "I tell you I know you not, whence ye are; depart from Me, all ye workers of iniquity." . . . Depart ye, therefore, every one to his own place; you see the openings into those caverns; enter, and there work shall be given each of you to do, and afterwards food according to your work; but should you refuse at present to enter, the demands of hunger will speedily compel you.'"

This, though not written for the purpose, bears plain testimony to the part which the opening of the Word to and through Swedenborg himself had in the diffusion of the light of the judgment.

And what were the effects of the judgment: Through the vast multitude of spirits gathered for harvest in the world of spirits the Gospel was preached anew with light from its Divine Author. As at His first coming, those who had done well welcomed the light and were gathered by it into its home, while those who had done evil fled from the light and were gathered unto their like in hell. Thus the atmosphere was cleared above and about men's souls; and from that time forward whenever the Word of God is read with simple heart, the light of heaven, which is none other than that of the Holy Spirit, flows into the mind and en-

THE APOCALYPSE EXPLAINED

ables it to see with some clearness the true purport of what is read. How truly does this explain the return of the Christian mind to the simple Gospel and the right understanding thereof!

The new heaven was formed of those gathered by the judgment into the fold of the Good Shepherd. The new earth, its child in the world, is being born and nurtured. But the holy city, the new Jerusalem, what is that? A city is the abode of a community of men, with separate dwellings but with common streets in which they walk in concert, and public grounds and buildings for common interests. The city of men's minds is a system of thought or, spiritually speaking, of doctrine, in which, while each mind has its peculiar abode, the general lines are held in common, with common centres for assembling, for common interests. And as in the centre of a city resides its government, so in the centre of a common cult or doctrine resides its object of worship, its Lord. So was it with the old Jerusalem, with the Law of God in its central most holy place. So is it with the new. The Holy City is to be the new Christian faith, the resurrected faith, as declared in the Gospel, and as newly called to our remembrance and made clear by the light of the Holy Spirit. It has no need of the sun [of earth], neither of the moon to shine in it; for the glory of God doth lighten it, and the Lamb is the light thereof.

For continuity of subject we have taken Swedenborg's Apocalypse Revealed in connection with his Apocalypse Explained. But after laying aside the latter he wrote various smaller works, of which he published The Doctrine of the New Jerusalem concerning the Lord, The Doctrine of the New Jerusalem concerning the Sacred Scripture, The Doctrine of Life for the New Jerusalem, and The Doctrine of the New Jerusalem concerning Faith; also a Continuation concerning the Final Judgment. These were but small treatises. In 1763 he published the larger work entitled " Angelic Wisdom concerning the Divine Love and the Divine Wisdom," and in the same or the next year that entitled " Angelic Wisdom concerning the Divine Providence." In these two most important works we find the spiritual philosophy of the New Church. Then came the Apocalypse Revealed, 1764–1766, followed in 1767 by "The Delights of Wisdom concerning Marriage Love." It

THE APOCALYPSE EXPLAINED

is noteworthy that this last named work was the first of his theological works to which the author attached his name, "By Emanuel Swedenborg, a Swede." But at the end of the volume he appends a "List of the Theological Works published by me," adding that they are still for sale at his printers and publishers in London. In the same style he affixed his name to the "Summary Exposition of the Doctrine of the New Church which is meant by the New Jerusalem in the Apocalypse." This was a small tract preliminary to his last important and crowning work entitled "The True Christian Religion, containing the entire theology of the New Church foretold by Daniel, chap. VII. 13, 14, and in the Apocalypse, XXI. 1, 2: by Emanuel Swedenborg, Servant of the Lord Jesus Christ." This appellation he told a friend that he had asked and received permission to affix. The original volume in Latin was published at Amsterdam in the year 1771, in a quarto of 541 pages.

This monumental work contains far more than a mere statement of the doctrine of the true Christian Church. It contains ample exposition of every particular, with confutation of all opposing doctrine. And between the chapters are *Memorabilia*

EMANUEL SWEDENBORG

of things seen and heard in the other world, especially of important discussions held in the world of spirits on the very points of doctrine considered in the chapters. We cannot better close this sketch of Swedenborg's theological works than with what he sets forth at the beginning of this last great work as "the face, gate, and summary" of this new Christian doctrine: —

"The faith of the New Heaven and the New Church in the Universal Form is this: — That the Lord from eternity, who is Jehovah, came into the world that He might subjugate the hells and glorify His Human; and that without this no mortal could have been saved; and that those are saved who believe in Him.

"It is said *in the universal form* because this is the universal of faith; and a universal of faith is that which will be in the whole and every part. It is a universal of faith that God is one in essence and in person, in whom is a Divine Trinity, and that He is the Lord God the Saviour Jesus Christ. It is a universal of faith that no mortal could have been saved unless the Lord had come into the world. It is a universal of faith that He came into the world that He might remove hell from man

THE APOCALYPSE EXPLAINED

and that He did remove it by means of combats against it and victories over it; thus He subjugated it and reduced it to order and under obedience to Himself. It is a universal of faith that He came into the world that He might glorify His Human which He assumed in the world, that is, might unite it to the Divine from which [it proceeded]; thus He holds hell in order and under obedience to Himself forever. Since this could not have been done but by means of temptations admitted into His Human, even to the last of them, and the last was the passion of the cross, therefore He underwent that temptation. These are the universals of faith concerning the Lord.

"The universal of faith on the part of man is that he should believe in the Lord; for by believing in Him conjunction with Him is effected, by which is salvation. To believe in Him is to have confidence that He saves; and because no one can have this confidence but he that lives well, therefore this also is meant by believing in Him."

Such is Swedenborg's own summary of the doctrine for the new age of the Christian Church — the "True Christian Religion" — which it was his mission to draw from the letter of the Word of God, under the guidance of the inner heavenly content revealed to him by the Holy Spirit. There is nothing new or strange in the doctrine, for it is simply that of our Lord Himself, as recorded in the Gospel, now first clearly and rationally understood. The difficulty with the common interpretations of the Gospel has been the lack of clear distinction between that in our Lord which was of man and that which was of God. This distinction is rightly understood only with experience in ourselves of the distinction between the natural man, which is of self and the world, and the spiritual man, which is of God and of heaven — a distinction of which Paul well warned us. The life natural to man, into which he is born, is centripetal, self-centred. The life of God which man is to receive for his own, in coming into the image and likeness of his Creator, is centrifugal, giving forth of itself endlessly for the blessing of others. Our Lord taught plainly the absolute necessity of conversion from the one life to the other in order to enter the kingdom of heaven. What has not been well understood is that within or above man's natural mind, with its necessary concern for himself, he has an inner or superior spiritual mind,

THE APOCALYPSE EXPLAINED

at first undeveloped, but capable of being opened and becoming lord of the house: not by any effort of the natural, but by the inflowing Divine life, when by instruction or experience the natural has been made willing to subside into its appointed place of humble service.

All this the Lord taught, not by words alone, but more emphatically by His own example, in Himself laying down the maternal human nature and living and speaking solely from the Divine Human nature within. It is this inner Divine Human life which He bade men recognize as the will of the Father, and in which He declared that whoever had seen and known Him, had seen and known the Father. In this He desired men also to understand that whatever they should be enabled to do of the Father's will, would be not of themselves, but of God. "Why callest thou Me good? None is good save **O**ne, that is, God." The comprehension of this Divine teaching was little possible to races just emerging from barbarism, or worse, from the profligacy of Roman civilization. What could they do in the way of renouncing their own will and accepting the Divine in its stead? For the time, therefore, it **was** permitted

EMANUEL SWEDENBORG

them to regard the Lord Jesus as a Divine Being distinct from the Father, retaining His maternal human nature, which for consistency has been determined in the Roman Church to have been itself Divinely immaculate. On this Rock of the Divine Human of our Lord the Christian Church has split and been shattered to pieces. The true understanding of this Corner-stone on which the Church is to be rebuilt is that the maternal human, after serving its temporary purpose as a recipient, and in itself being rejected, no longer existed. But the Divine Life which had in this maternal human entered fully into the life of men, had thereby acquired a perpetual Divine Human presence with man, in which it became God-with-us, our known Father in heaven.

IX

MANNER OF LIFE IN LATER PERIOD

THE outward manner of life of one whose inner life is passed in open communication with spirits and angels, cannot but be of interest. Happily in Swedenborg's case we are not without abundant information. In 1748 at sixty years of age he went to London to put to press the first volume of the Arcana, and there for similar purpose he made his home much of the time until his death, twenty-four years later. In 1750 John Lewis, his publisher, in the advertisement of the second volume of the Arcana said —

"Though the author of the *Arcana Cœlestia* is undoubtedly a very learned and great man, and his works highly esteemed by the *literati*, yet he is no less distinguished for his modesty than for his great talents, so that he will not suffer his name to be made public. But though I am positively forbid to discover that, yet I hope he will excuse me if I venture to mention his benign and generous qualities. How he bestowed his time and labors in former years I am not certainly informed, though I have heard by those who have been long acquainted with him that they were employed in the same manner as I am going to relate; but what I have been an eye-witness to, I can declare with certain truth; and therefore I do aver that this gentleman, with indefatigable pains and labor, spent one whole year in studying and writing the first volume of the *Arcana Cœlestia*, was at the expense of two hundred pounds to print it, and also advanced two hundred pounds more for the printing of this second volume; and when he had done this, he gave express orders that all the money that should arise in the sale of this large work should be given toward the charge of the propagation of the Gospel. He is so far from desiring to make a gain of his labors, that he will not receive one farthing back of the four hundred pounds he has expended; and for that reason his works will come exceedingly cheap to the public."

In the spring of 1750 Swedenborg returned again to Stockholm, having spent the intervening time partly in London, but mostly in Holland. In Stockholm he remained, tending his garden and busily employed on the Arcana. We hear no

MANNER OF LIFE IN LATER PERIOD

more of him at the College of Mines, but for some time yet we have an occasional paper presented to the Diet. A paper of much importance had been presented by him in 1734, in opposition to a party plan of declaring war against Russia, which is supposed to have had great weight in maintaining peace at that time. A fragment of a memorial addressed by him to the Diet in 1755 urges the necessity of limiting the distillation of whiskey, "that is, if the consumption of the whiskey cannot be done away with altogether, which would be more desirable for the country's welfare and morality than all the income which could be realized from so pernicious a drink." In addition, the memorial urges a recall of the power granted to the Bank to grant loans on all property in the country, which he regarded as one of the causes of the bankruptcy into which it was drifting. By these means Swedenborg hoped a check might be put on the drain from the country, as shown by the excess of imports over exports, and the balance of trade be restored in its favor.

In 1760 also, on occasion of a financial panic in Sweden, as a member of a committee on Finance, he presented to the Diet a memorial showing the necessity of curtailing the issue by the Bank, of loans on any other property than gold and silver; of gradually diminishing the amount of certificates of indebtedness that had been issued on other property, by requiring the debtors to pay each year a certain percentage of their debt in addition to the interest; of gradual redemption by the Bank of all other notes than those payable in coin; of prohibiting for the time all exportation of copper, and requiring the Bank to hoard it in anticipation of resumption; of abolishing the monopoly of the Iron-Office; and finally of farming out the distillation of whiskey, as a means of revenue, if the consumption of the pernicious drink could not be done away with altogether.

Not long after, in refutation of some charges against the Government, Swedenborg addressed the Diet in these terms: —

"Every human being is inclined by nature, and nothing is easier and pleasanter for him to do than to find faults in others, and to pass an unfavorable judgment upon them, inasmuch as all of us are by nature inclined to see the mote in our brother's eye and not to see the beam in our own eyes; moreover we are apt to strain out a gnat and **to**

MANNER OF LIFE IN LATER PERIOD

swallow a camel. All proud and evil-disposed men place their prudence in finding fault with and blaming others; and all generous and truly Christian souls place their prudence in judging all things according to circumstances, and hence in excusing such faults as may have arisen from weakness, and in inveighing against such evils as may have been done on purpose. The same also happens in a general way in that which concerns governments: faults, numberless faults may be found in all, so that volumes might be filled with them. Should I undertake to make known all the mistakes of which I have heard, and which I know from my own experience to have happened in England and Holland to the detriment of justice and the public good, I believe I might fill a whole book with lamentations; when, nevertheless, those governments, together with our own in Sweden, are the very best in Europe, as every inhabitant, notwithstanding all the shortcomings which happen there, is safe in his life and property, and no one is a slave, but they are all free men. The Honorable Houses of the Diet will allow me to go still higher: if in this world there should exist a heavenly government, consisting of men who had an angelic disposition, there would nevertheless be in it faults caused by weakness, together with other shortcomings; and if these were ferreted out, reported, and exaggerated, this government too might be undermined by calumny, and thereby gradually a desire might be raised among the well-disposed to change and destroy it. The best government, and that which is most wisely arranged, is our own government in Sweden; inasmuch as all things are connected here as in a chain, and are joined together for the purpose of administering justice from the highest leader to the lowest citizen."

Swedenborg spoke from much experience, having been in friendly relations with several kings and queens, an officer of the government thirty years in the College of Mines, and being in the Diet of the party which curtailed the royal power, retaining the supreme control in the Houses of the Diet themselves. This was in 1762. The next year his views prevailed and his first measure was passed, forbidding bank loans on movable property. The year after, however, against Swedenborg's advice, a too sudden and radical measure was adopted and the whole ground was lost.

MANNER OF LIFE IN LATER PERIOD

Another matter that gave him concern about this time was the controversy between the Court and the Diet on behalf of the people. The latter party under the lead of Count Höpken and other senators had sustained the alliance of Sweden with France, against the wishes of the Royal family, which was allied to that of Prussia. The war that ensued was unfortunate, and Höpken and two colleagues were obliged to resign. In 1761 Swedenborg memorialized the Diet in strong terms, urging the necessity of maintaining intact the government, at once free and conservative, which they had hitherto enjoyed, resisting the encroachments of the Court, backed by that of Prussia, itself under the influence of intriguing Papacy, and maintaining sacred their alliance with France. In this view he strongly advised the restoration of Höpken and his colleagues, as tried and faithful servants of Sweden — advice that was afterward followed.

As stated by a Swedish authority —

"Up to the time of his extreme old age Swedenborg interested himself in the administrative, financial, and political affairs of his country. As a member of the House of Nobles, he was an independent member, supporting whatever he saw to be worthy of his own position and to be right and generally useful, without allowing himself to be influenced by the right or the left side. Like every true friend of liberty, he was opposed alike to despotism and to anarchy. His entrance into the House of Nobles was contemporaneous with the reëstablishment of freedom in Sweden. During his childhood and youth he had witnessed the misfortunes into which an unlimited monarchy had precipitated his country. He himself had seen the misery and distress which a war of eighteen years' duration, with dearly-bought victories and bloody defeats, with decimated armies and bankrupt finances, attended by pestilence and famine, had brought upon it. Need we wonder, then, that Swedenborg was in favor of a constitution which set bounds to the arbitrary power and whims of a hitherto unlimited monarchy; which prevented the dissolution of the country, and gradually changed discontent into satisfaction, at least among the majority of its citizens? Swedenborg enjoyed the good fortune envied by many, of having been able during half a century to influence by his vote the resolutions passed for the

MANNER OF LIFE IN LATER PERIOD

welfare of his country, and of not giving up his place in the House of Nobles before the year 1772, when death closed his eyes to the darkened prospects with which a change in the administration threatened Sweden's independence. He thus belonged to the whole of that period of freedom which is valued so highly by many, and is made light of by others. With that period his political career began and ended."[1]

Thus it appears that Swedenborg, after as before his introduction into his spiritual office and into visible heavenly companionship, was alive to the important questions of the day to which he was called by love for his country and his duty as a member of its Diet. With spiritual eyes open to all his spiritual surroundings, his natural eyes were wide open also to all real needs of this world. He lived much alone, as his constant absorbing labors required, but he was not a recluse. He had many friends among statesmen and men of learning, with whom he enjoyed pleasant intercourse. His garden was his solace, and he took much pleasure in meeting young children, whom he loved to make happy. Of his friendly relations

[1] *Nya Kyrkan, i, Sverige*, part ii, p. 48.

EMANUEL SWEDENBORG

in his own country he wrote in answer to the inquiries of an English friend in 1769 —

"Moreover, all the bishops of my native country, who are ten in number, and also the sixteen senators, and the rest of those highest in office, entertain feelings of affection for me; from their affection they honor me, and I live with them on terms of familiarity, as a friend among friends — the reason of which is that they know I am in company with angels. Even the King and the Queen and the three princes, their sons, show me great favor. I was invited once by the King and Queen to dine with them at their own table, which honor is generally accorded only to those who are highest in office; subsequently the Crown Prince granted me the same favor. They all desire me to return home; wherefore I am far from apprehending in my own country that persecution which you fear, and against which in your letter you desire in so friendly a manner to provide; and if they choose to persecute me elsewhere, it can do me no harm."

Of the esteem in which Swedenborg was held in Sweden the following letter gives a pleasing account. It was written by Count Anders Johan

MANNER OF LIFE IN LATER PERIOD

Von Höpken,[1] holding office under the Swedish Government equivalent to Prime Minister, to his friend General Tuxen, another friend of Swedenborg's, who held important office under the Danish Government at Elsinore.

"I have not only known him these two and forty years, but also, some time since, daily frequented his company. A man who like me has lived long in the world, and even in an extensive career of life, must have had numerous opportunities of knowing men as to their virtues or vices, their weakness or strength; and in consequence thereof I do not recollect to have known any man of more uniformly virtuous character than Swedenborg — always contented, never fretful or morose, though throughout his life his soul was occupied with sublime thoughts and speculations. He was a true philosopher and lived like one; he labored diligently and lived frugally without sordidness; he travelled continually, and his travels cost him no more than if he had lived at home. He was gifted with a most happy genius and a fitness for every science, which made him shine

---

[1] Called in the Swedish Biographical Dictionary "The Swedish Tacitus."

EMANUEL SWEDENBORG

in all those which he embraced. He was without contradiction the most learned man in my country. In his youth he was a great poet : I have in my possession some remnants of his Latin poetry which Ovid would not have been ashamed to own. In his middle age his Latin was in an easy, elegant, and ornamental style; in his latter years it was equally clear, but less elegant after he had turned his thoughts to spiritual subjects. He was well acquainted with Hebrew and Greek, an able and profound mathematician, a happy mechanician, of which he gave proof in Norway, where by an easy and simple method he transported the largest galleys over high mountains and rocks to a gulf where the Danish fleet was stationed. . . . He possessed a sound judgment upon all occasions; he saw everything clearly and expressed himself well on every subject. The most solid memorials and the best penned at the Diet of 1761 on matters of finance, were presented by him. . . .

"I once represented in rather a serious manner to this venerable man, that I thought he would do better not to mix with his beautiful writings so many 'memorable relations,' or things heard and

MANNER OF LIFE IN LATER PERIOD

seen in the spiritual world concerning the states of men after death, of which ignorance makes a jest and derision. But he answered me that this did not depend on him; that he was too old to sport with spiritual things, and too much concerned for his eternal happiness to yield to such foolish notions; assuring me on his hopes of salvation that imagination produced in him none of his revelations, which were true and from what he had heard and seen."

In another letter Count Höpken recurs to the same point: speaking of a certain clergyman, he says —

"He was by no means a Swedenborgian, for he did not understand his 'memorable relations'; and I could wish the happy deceased had left them out, as they may prevent infidelity from approaching his doctrines. I represented to him these inconveniences; but he said that he was commanded to declare what he had seen in the other world; and he related it as a proof that he did not reveal his own thoughts, but that they came from above. As for the rest, I find in his system a simplicity and gradation and such a spirit as the work of God in nature everywhere proves and exhibits; for

EMANUEL SWEDENBORG

whatever man creates is complicated, labored, and subject to vicissitude."

In a letter to another friend, still to the same point, the Count says—

"There are two circumstances in the doctrine and writings of Swedenborg. The first is his 'memorable relations.' Of these I cannot judge, not having had any spiritual intercourse myself, by which to judge of his assertions either approvingly or disapprovingly; but they cannot appear more extraordinary than the Apocalypse of John, and other similar relations in the Bible. The second is his tenets of doctrine. Of these I can judge: they are excellent, irrefutable, and the best that ever were taught, promoting the happiest social life. I know that Swedenborg wrote his *memorabilia bonâ fide*. . . .

"I have sometimes told the King that if ever a new colony were to be formed, no religion could be better, as the prevailing and established one, than that developed by Swedenborg from the Sacred Scriptures, and this for the two following reasons: First, this religion, in preference to and in a higher degree than any other, must produce the most honest and industrious subjects; for it

MANNER OF LIFE IN LATER PERIOD

properly places the worship of God in uses. Second, it causes least fear of death, as this religion regards death merely as a transition from one state to another, from a worse to a better situation; nay, upon his principles I look upon death as being of hardly any greater moment than drinking a glass of water. I have been convinced of the truth of Swedenborg's doctrine from these arguments in particular, namely, that ONE is the author of everything, and that a separate person is not the Creator, and another the Author of religion; that there are degrees in everything and these subsisting to eternity; the history of creation is unaccountable unless explained in the spiritual sense. We may say of the religion which Swedenborg has developed in his writings from the Word of God, with Gamaliel: 'If it be of God, it cannot be overthrown; but if it be of man, it will come to nought.'"

That Swedenborg on his part held Höpken in high esteem is shown by the memorials to the Diet in his favor, to which we have already alluded. We will take our leave of the Count in copying his statement of the "Truthful account made by the late Queen Dowager":—

EMANUEL SWEDENBORG

"Swedenborg was one day at a court reception. Her Majesty [the Queen Dowager Louisa Ulrica] asked him about different things in the other life, and lastly whether he had seen or talked with her brother, the Prince Royal of Prussia. He answered, 'No.' Her Majesty then requested him to ask after him, and to give him her greeting, which Swedenborg promised to do. I doubt whether the Queen meant anything serious by it. At the next reception Swedenborg again appeared at court; and while the Queen was in the so-called white room, surrounded by her ladies of honor, he came boldly in and approached her Majesty, who no longer remembered the commission she had given him a week before. Swedenborg not only greeted her from her brother, but also gave her his apologies for not having answered her last letter; he also wished to do so now through Swedenborg, which he accordingly did. The Queen was greatly overcome, and said, 'No one except God knows this secret.'

"The reason why the Queen never adverted to this before, was that she did not wish any one in Sweden to believe that during a war with Prussia she had carried on a correspondence in the

MANNER OF LIFE IN LATER PERIOD

enemy's country. The same caution her Majesty exercised during her last visit to Berlin. When she was asked about this transaction, which had been printed in a German paper, she did not answer."

The same story comes to us through many different channels, to substantially the same effect. The account given by Mr. Springer, as from Swedenborg himself, contains a variation quite likely to be true:—

"The Queen of Sweden had written letters to her brother, a Prince of Prussia; and having no answers, she doubted whether he had received them or not. The Baron [Swedenborg] at that time had converse with the Queen, and her brother had died in Prussia. She was very desirous to know if he had received the letters. She consulted the Baron, who said he would inform her in a few days. He did so, and told her he had received them and was going to answer them, and that in an escritoire of the Prince was a letter unfinished intended for her; but he was taken ill and died. She sent to the King of Prussia, and it was as the Baron had declared: the King sent the unfinished letter."

EMANUEL SWEDENBORG

The Prince of Prussia referred to was Augustus William, brother to Frederic II and to the Queen Louisa Ulrica, wife of Adolphus Frederic, King of Sweden from 1751 to 1771. It is amusingly told, on the authority of the wife of Swedenborg's gardener, that " for days following the occurrence carriages stopped before the door of her master, from which the first gentlemen of the kingdom alighted, who desired to know the secret of which the Queen was so much frightened; but her master, faithful to his promise, refused to tell it."

Christopher Springer, whose statement we have just quoted, was a Swede, and long a friend of Swedenborg, both in their own country and in London, where for political reasons he resided many years. He had been prominent in public affairs at home, and became the confidential agent of the English Government in all that concerned Swedish matters, being employed in bringing about peace between Sweden and Frederick the Great in 1762. In London he was regarded as the father of the Swedes, and was applied to for all aid and information. In answer to inquiries about Swedenborg, after his decease, Mr. Springer said —

MANNER OF LIFE IN LATER PERIOD

"His father, Jesper Swedberg, was Bishop of Skara, a man of great learning; but this Emanuel Swedenborg received richer endowments from God. His knowledge as well as his sincerity was great. He was constant in friendship, extremely frugal in his diet, and plain in his dress. His usual food was coffee with milk, and bread and butter; sometimes, however, he partook of a little fish, and only at rare intervals ate meat; and he never drank above two glasses of wine. . . .

"Two or three weeks before his decease . . . I asked him when he believed that the New Jerusalem, or the New Church of God, would manifest itself, and whether this manifestation would take place in the four quarters of the world. His answer was that no mortal and not even the celestial angels could predict the time; that it was solely in the will of God. 'Read,' said he, 'the Book of Revelation xxi. 2, and Zechariah xiv. 9, and you will see there that the New Jerusalem will undoubtedly manifest itself to the whole earth.' . . .

"Fifteen years ago [in 1766] Swedenborg set out for Sweden, and asked me to procure a good captain for him, which I did. I contracted with one whose name was Dixon. . . . When the captain of the vessel called for Swedenborg, I took leave of him and wished him a happy journey. Having then asked the captain if he had a good supply of provisions on board, he answered me that he had as much as would be required. Swedenborg then observed, 'My friend, we have not need of a great quantity; for this day week we shall, by the aid of God, enter into the port of Stockholm at two o'clock.' On Captain Dixon's return, he related to me that this happened exactly as Swedenborg had foretold.

"Two years afterward Swedenborg returned to London, where we continued our former friendship. He told me that he had sent his works to the bishops of Sweden, but without result, and that they had received him with the same indifference that he had experienced from the bishops in England. What a remarkable change I noticed among the bishops in London! I had witnessed myself with what coldness he was received by them before his departure for Sweden, and I saw that on his return he was received by them with the greatest civility. I asked him how this change could have come, when he answered, 'God

MANNER OF LIFE IN LATER PERIOD

knows the time when His Church ought to commence.' . . .

"As to what relates to myself, I cannot give you a reason for the great friendship Swedenborg entertained for me, who am not a learned man. It is true, we were good friends in Sweden; but that this friendship between us should have become as constant as it has been, I never expected.

"All that he had told me of my deceased friends and enemies, and all of the secrets I had with them, is almost past belief. He even explained to me in what manner peace was concluded between Sweden and the King of Prussia; and he praised my conduct on that occasion He even specified the three high personages whose services I made use of at that time; which was nevertheless a profound secret between us. On asking him how it was possible for him to obtain such information, and who had discovered it to him, he replied, 'Who informed me about your affair with Count Claes Ekeblad? You cannot deny that what I have told you is true. Continue,' he added, ' to merit his reproaches [for refusing a great bribe]; depart not from the good way either for honors or money; but, on the contrary, continue as constant therein as you have hitherto, and you will prosper.'"

John Christian Cuno, soldier, poet, and merchant, of Amsterdam, left a manuscript autobiography, in which he has much to say of Swedenborg: —

"I must remain faithful to a promise made last year, and begin by giving an account of the most singular saint who has ever lived, Mr. Emanuel Swedenborg. As nothing concerns me more in this world than the worship of God, and as I found interspersed in the last work of that man such strange and singular things, I was naturally impelled by an irresistible curiosity to make the acquaintance of the author. . . .

"The Christian worship of God is subject to this sad calamity in this world, that attacks are made upon it either by arrogant fools who call themselves strong-minded, or by visionaries; the latter rendering it ridiculous sometimes without wishing to do so, but the former endeavoring to do so with all their power. The learned Mr. Swedenborg cannot be classed among the freethinkers and enemies of the Christian religion; for he writes with the greatest reverence for God and His Word.

MANNER OF LIFE IN LATER PERIOD

He has impressed upon me the most profound reverence for the adorable Saviour of the world, and his entire system of doctrine is based upon His Divinity. . . .

"I scarcely believe that he has any enemies; at all events he could not have made them by the innocent, even sainted, tenor of his life; and should he have them, it would be impossible for them, as well as for the scoffers who examine closely all modes of life different from their own, to discover anything in him which they could justly find fault with, or even calumniate. . . .

"My first acquaintance with him dates from November 4, 1768, when I happened to meet him in the French book-shop of Mr. François Changuion. The old gentleman speaks both French and High-German, yet not very readily. Besides, he is afflicted with the natural infirmity of stammering; yet at one time more than at another. Our first meeting was pleasing and sympathetic. He permitted me to call upon him at his own house, which I did on the following Sunday; and I continued to do so almost every Sunday, after attending church in the morning. He lodged near our old church in Kälbergasse [Amsterdam], where he

EMANUEL SWEDENBORG

had engaged two comfortable rooms. One of my first questions was whether he had no male attendant to wait upon him in his old age, and to accompany him on his journeys. He answered that he needed no one to look after him, because his angel was ever with him, and conversed and held communication with him. If another man had uttered these words, he would have made me laugh; but I never thought of laughing when this venerable man, eighty-one years old, told me this — he looked far too innocent; and when he gazed on me with his smiling blue eyes, which he always did in conversing with me, it was as if truth itself was speaking from them. I often noticed with surprise how scoffers, who had made their way into large companies where I had taken him, and whose purpose it had been to make fun of the old gentleman, forgot all their laughter and their intended scoffing; and how they stood agape and listened to the most singular things which he, like an openhearted child, told about the spiritual world, without reserve and with full confidence. It almost seemed as if his eyes possessed the faculty of imposing silence on every one.

"He lived with simple burgher folks, who kept

MANNER OF LIFE IN LATER PERIOD

a shop in which they sold chintz, muslin, handkerchiefs, and the like, and who had quite a number of little children. I inquired of the landlady whether the old gentleman did not require very much attention. She answered, ' He scarcely requires any; the servant has nothing to do for him except in the morning to lay the fire for him in the fireplace. Every evening he goes to bed at seven, and gets up in the morning at eight. We do not trouble ourselves any more about him. During the day he keeps up the fire himself, and on going to bed takes great care lest the fire should do any damage. He dresses and undresses himself alone, and waits upon himself in everything; so that we scarcely know whether there is any one in the house or not. I should like him to be with us during the rest of his life. My children will miss him most; for he never goes out without bringing them home sweets: the little rogues also dote on the old gentleman so much that they prefer him to their own parents.' . . .

"It soon became known in town that I associated with this remarkable man, and everybody troubled me to give them an opportunity of making his acquaintance. I advised the people to do

EMANUEL SWEDENBORG

as I had done, and to call upon him, because he willingly conversed with every honest man. Mr. Swedenborg moves in the world with great tact, and knows how to address the high as well as the low. . . .

"Once, at the urgent request of my friend, Mr. Nicolam Konauw, I agreed to bring him to dinner. The old gentleman consented and was prepared at once to go. Mr. Konauw sent his carriage for us. On presenting ourselves to Madame, we found among other guests the two Misses Hoog, who had been highly educated and had been introduced, beyond the common sphere of woman, into the higher, especially the philosophical sciences. Mr. Swedenborg's deportment was exquisitely refined and gallant. When dinner was announced, I offered my hand to the hostess, and quickly our young man of eighty-one years had put on his gloves and presented his hand to Mademoiselle Hoog, in doing which he looked uncommonly well. Whenever he was invited out, he dressed properly and becomingly in black velvet; but ordinarily he wore a brown coat and black trousers. . . .

"I shall never forget, as long as I live, the

MANNER OF LIFE IN LATER PERIOD

leave which he took of me in my own house. It seemed to me as if this truly venerable old man was much more eloquent this last time, and spoke differently from what I ever heard him speak before. He admonished me to continue in goodness and to acknowledge the Lord for my God. 'If it please God, I shall once more come to you in Amsterdam; for I love you.' 'O my worthy Mr. Swedenborg,' I interrupted him, 'this will probably not take place in this world; for I, at least, do not attribute to myself a long life.' 'This you cannot know,' he continued, 'we are obliged to remain as long in the world as the Divine providence and wisdom sees fit. If any one is conjoined with the Lord, he has a foretaste of the eternal life in this world; and if he has this, he no longer cares so much about this transitory life. Believe me, if I knew that the Lord would call me to Himself to-morrow, I would summon the musicians to-day, in order to be once more really gay in this world.' In order to feel what I felt then, you would have had to hear the old man say this, in his second childhood. This time also he looked so innocent and so joyful out of his eyes as I had never seen him look before. I did not interrupt him, and was as it were dumb with astonishment He then saw a Bible lying on my desk, and while I was thus gazing quietly before me and he could easily see the state of my mind, he took the book and opened it at this passage — 1 John v. 20, 21. 'Read these words,' he said, and then closed the book again, 'but that you may not forget them, I will rather put them down for you;' and in saying these words he dipped the pen in order to write the reference on the leaf which is preserved here; his hand however trembled, as may be seen from the figure 1. This I could not bear, and so I asked him in a friendly manner to mention the passage to me. I then put down the reference myself. As soon as I had done so, he arose. 'The time now approaches,' he said, 'when I must take leave of my other friends.' He then embraced and kissed me most heartily.

"As soon as he had left, I read the passage which he had recommended to me. It read thus: 'But we know that the Son of God has come, and hath given us an understanding that we may know Him that is true, and we are in Him that is true, even in His Son, Jesus Christ. This is

MANNER OF LIFE IN LATER PERIOD

the true God, and eternal life. Little children, keep yourselves from idols. Amen.'"

In 1770 Cuno again noted in his memoirs —

"Last year I gave my readers many sheets to read respecting my dear old Swedenborg; but I am by no means done yet with this singular man, and as long as my eyes remain open, I shall not so easily turn them away from him. I still hear news concerning him from Sweden, nay, a short time ago he desired to be remembered to me, and sent me word that he hoped to embrace me this summer. The clergy have made an assault upon him with all their power, but they could not do him any harm, because those high in authority, even, it is said, the King and the Queen, love him."

In his "Theory of Pneumatology" J. H. Jung-Stilling — whose name is cited in Kürtz's "Church History" among the five most brilliant and best known names of the faithful sons of the Church who withstood the rationalistic spirit of the age — says —

"As so very much has been written both for and against this extraordinary man, I consider it my duty to make known the pure truth respecting

EMANUEL SWEDENBORG

him, since I have had an opportunity of knowing it pure and uncontaminated."

After declaring that Swedenborg was no impostor, but a pious Christian man, and referring to the "three proofs generally known that he had actually intercourse with spirits," Stilling continues —

"But I must add here a fourth experimental proof which has not been made public before, and which is fully as important as any of the foregoing. I can vouch for the truth of it with the greatest certainty.

"About the year 1770 there was a merchant in Elberfeld with whom during seven years of my residence there I lived in close intimacy. He was a strict mystic in the purest sense. He spoke little, but what he said was like golden fruit on a salver of silver. He would not have dared for all the world knowingly to tell a falsehood. This friend of mine, who has long ago left this world for a better, related to me the following story: —

"His business required him to take a journey to Amsterdam, where Swedenborg at that time resided; and having heard and read much of this singular man, he formed the intention of visiting

MANNER OF LIFE IN LATER PERIOD

him and becoming better acquainted with him. He therefore called upon him, and found a very venerable-looking, friendly old man, who received him politely and requested him to be seated, whereupon the following conversation began:—

"*Merchant.* 'Having been called hither by business, I could not deny myself the honor, Sir, of paying my respects to you: your writings have caused me to regard you as a very remarkable man.'

"*Swedenborg.* 'May I ask you where you are from?'

"*M.* 'I am from Elberfeld, in the Duchy of Berg. Your writings contain so much that is beautiful and edifying, that they have made a deep impression on me; but the source from which you derive them is so extraordinary, so strange and uncommon, that you will perhaps not take it amiss of a sincere friend of truth if he desire incontestable proofs that you really have intercourse with the spiritual world.'

"*S.* 'It would be very unreasonable if I took it amiss; but I think I have given sufficient proofs, which cannot be contradicted.'

"*M.* 'Are these the well-known ones, respect-

EMANUEL SWEDENBORG

ing the Queen, the fire in Stockholm, and the receipt?'

"S. 'Yes, those are they, and they are true.'

"M. 'And yet many objections are brought against them. Might I venture to propose that you give me a similar proof?'

"S. 'Why not? Most willingly.'

"M. 'I had formerly a friend who studied Divinity at Duisburg, where he fell into consumption, of which he died. I visited this friend a short time before his decease; we conversed together on an important topic: could you learn from him what was the subject of our discourse?'

"S. 'We will see. What was the name of your friend?'

"The merchant told his name.

"S. 'How long do you remain here?'

"M. 'About eight or ten days.'

"S. 'Call upon me again in a few days. I will see if I can find your friend.'

"The merchant took his leave and despatched his business. Some days afterward he went again to Swedenborg, full of expectation. The old gentleman met him with a smile and said — 'I have spoken with your friend; the subject of your dis-

MANNER OF LIFE IN LATER PERIOD

course was *the restitution of all things*.' He then related to the merchant with the greatest precision what he and what his deceased friend had maintained. My friend turned pale, for this proof was powerful and invincible. He inquired further —'How fares it with my friend? Is he in a state of blessedness?' Swedenborg answered, 'No, he is not in heaven yet; he is still in hades, and torments himself continually with the idea of the restitution of all things.' This answer caused my friend the greatest astonishment. He exclaimed—'My God! what, in the other world?' Swedenborg replied— 'Certainly, a man takes with him his favorite inclination and opinions, and it is very difficult to be divested of them: we ought therefore to lay them aside here.' My friend took his leave of this remarkable man perfectly convinced, and returned back to Elberfeld. . . . That Swedenborg for many years had frequent intercourse with the inhabitants of the spiritual world, is not subject to any doubt, but is a settled fact."

Another statement given by Jung-Stilling, as he had it from "a certain beloved friend for many years, who is far advanced in Christianity," **is as follows**:—

EMANUEL SWEDENBORG

"In the year 1762, on the very day when Peter III of Russia died, Swedenborg was present with me [a God-fearing friend of Stilling's friend] at a party in Amsterdam. In the middle of the conversation his physiognomy changed, and it was evident that his soul was no longer present in him and that something was taking place with him. As soon as he recovered, he was asked what had happened. At first he would not speak out; but after being repeatedly urged, he said, 'Now, at this very hour, the Emperor Peter III has died in prison'—explaining the nature of his death [strangled by order of the Empress]. 'Gentlemen, will you please make a note of this day, in order that you may compare it with the announcement of his death which will appear in the newspaper?' The papers soon after announced the death of the Emperor, which had taken place on the very same day. . . .

"Such is the account of my friend; if any one doubts this statement, it is a proof that he has no sense of what is called historical faith and its grounds, and that he believes only what he himself hears and sees."

And yet Jung-Stilling himself preferred attri-

MANNER OF LIFE IN LATER PERIOD

buting Swedenborg's communication with the other world to somnambulism and a state of ecstasy in which spirits spoke through him — a notion not at all consistent with the fact that Swedenborg never laid aside his own reason and the control of his speech and acts. These illustrations of this open communication we quote, not as proofs to convince the incredulous — no second-hand testimony can do that — but as a part of Swedenborg's daily life which cannot fairly be omitted, and which indeed is necessary to complete our understanding of his being present in both worlds at once. As such they serve as confirmation to those who recognize the spiritual truths which this communication was given to reveal.

Of the three proofs to which Jung-Stilling referred, we have already seen the story of Queen Ulrica and her brother. The second is of the fire in Stockholm known to Swedenborg at Gottenburg; and the third is of a mislaid receipt. Of these occurrences Swedenborg himself says, in a letter to Venator, minister of the Landgrave of Hesse-Darmstadt —

"These must by no means be regarded as

miracles; for they are simply testimonies that **I** have been introduced by the Lord into the spiritual world and have intercourse and converse there with angels and spirits, in order that the Church, which has hitherto remained in ignorance concerning that world, may know that heaven and hell really exist, and that man lives after death a man as before; and that thus no more doubts may flow into his mind in respect to his **immortality**."

The occurrence of the Stockholm fire is variously related. Immanuel Kant's account, gathered by him with great care for a correspondent, seems most complete and trustworthy, with **R. L. Tafel's** correction of the date. Says Kant —

"The following occurrence appears to me to have the greatest weight of proof, and to place the assertion respecting Swedenborg's extraordinary gift beyond all possibility of doubt:—

"In the year 1759, toward the end of July, on Saturday at four o'clock P. M., Swedenborg arrived at Gottenburg from England, when **Mr.** William Castel invited him to his house, together with **a** party of fifteen persons. About six o'clock Swedenborg went out, and returned to the com-

MANNER OF LIFE IN LATER PERIOD

pany quite pale and alarmed. He said that a dangerous fire had just broken out in Stockholm, in the Södermalm (Gottenburg is about three hundred miles from Stockholm), and it was spreading very fast. He was restless and went out often. He said that the house of one of his friends, whom he named, was already in ashes, and his own was in danger. At eight o'clock, after he had been out again, he joyfully exclaimed, 'Thank God! the fire is extinguished, the third door from my house.' The news occasioned great commotion throughout the whole city, but particularly amongst the company in which he was. It was announced to the governor the same evening. On Sunday morning Swedenborg was summoned to the governor, who questioned him concerning the disaster. Swedenborg described the fire precisely — how it had begun, and how it had continued, and in what manner it had ceased. On the same day the news spread through the city and, as the governor had thought it worthy of attention, the consternation was considerably increased, because many were in trouble, on account of their friends and property which might have been involved in the disaster. On Monday evening a messenger arrived at Gottenburg, who was despatched by the Board of Trade during the time of the fire. In the letters brought by him the fire was described precisely in the manner stated by Swedenborg. On Tuesday morning the royal courier arrived at the governor's with the melancholy intelligence of the fire, of the loss which it had occasioned, and of the houses it had damaged and ruined, not in the least differing from that which Swedenborg had given at the very time when it happened; for the fire was extinguished at eight o'clock."

From many different accounts of the lost receipt, agreeing in substance, we select again that of Kant, confirmed as it is in all essential particulars by the secretary of the legation and executor of the estate: —

"Madame Marteville, the widow of the Dutch Ambassador in Stockholm, some time after the death of her husband, was called upon by Croon, a goldsmith, to pay for a silver service which her husband had purchased from him. The widow was convinced that her late husband had been much too precise and orderly not to have paid this debt, yet she was unable to find the receipt.

MANNER OF LIFE IN LATER PERIOD

In her sorrow, and because the amount was considerable, she requested Mr. Swedenborg to call at her house. After apologizing to him for troubling him, she said that if, as all people say, he possessed the extraordinary gift of conversing with the souls of the departed, he would perhaps have the kindness to ask her husband how it was about the silver service. Swedenborg did not at all object to comply with her request. Three days afterward the said lady had company at her house for coffee. Swedenborg called, and in his cool way informed her that he had conversed with her husband. The debt had been paid seven months before his decease, and the receipt was in a bureau in the room up-stairs. The lady replied that the bureau had been quite cleared out, and that the receipt was not found among all the papers. Swedenborg said that her husband had described to him how, after pulling out the left-hand drawer, a board would appear which required to be drawn out, when a secret compartment would be disclosed, containing his private Dutch correspondence, as well as the receipt. Upon hearing this description the whole company rose and accompanied the lady into the room up-stairs.

EMANUEL SWEDENBORG

The bureau was opened; they did as they were directed; the compartment was found, of which no one had known before; and to the great astonishment of all, the papers were discovered there in accordance with his description."

X

LATER PERIOD OF LIFE : CONCLUSION

ANOTHER of the five faithful sons of the Church named by Kürtz was Oetinger, called by him "the magus of the south," "the first representative of a theology of the future." It is interesting to note that Swedenborg's relations of things heard and seen in the other world, which Höpken would have wished omitted, were to Oetinger the most attractive part of his theological works, for the reason perhaps that his spiritual interpretations of the prophecies of Scripture were at variance with Oetinger's conception of their literal fulfilment. With his own works Oetinger published translations of intermediate chapters in Swedenborg's Arcana, under the following introduction:—

"I herewith present to the reader something rare, which God has given us to know in the present times. It is profitable to compare unusual things with those to which we are accustomed; but in doing so it is necessary sometimes to keep back our judgment until we are able to take in the

EMANUEL SWEDENBORG

whole matter. The infidelity which is rife now in the world has induced God to make use of a celebrated philosopher in order to communicate to us heavenly information. Mathematics have checked the imagination of this philosopher; wherefore it will not do to say that he reports mere imaginations. Experimental facts are not imaginations. These experiences are due to the influx of heavenly intelligence by the command of the Lord. Should any one say, 'We have Moses and the Prophets,' he may read what follows or not, just as he pleases. Still, a person anxious to improve himself ought not to forego any opportunity by which he may become acquainted with new light offered to him by truth. Swedenborg, a distinguished Assessor of the College of Mines in Sweden, wrote a large work in folio, which is most costly. This I call Earthly Philosophy in contradistinction to the following, which is of a heavenly origin, and which he has published in thirteen works that are still more valuable. Should you find therein propositions which appear objectionable, remember the twelve Ephesians in the Acts, xix. 21, who 'had not so much as heard whether there be any Holy Ghost,' and nevertheless were thought worthy at

LATER PERIOD OF LIFE : CONCLUSION

once to receive the Holy Spirit, notwithstanding they were ignorant of one of the chief grounds of faith, and opposed to the Scripture. Does not Swedenborg place the Scripture higher than any one else? and does he not wish to have all experiences judged thereby? Is not all he says well connected? And does he not appeal to many witnesses?"

Referring to the first volume of the same philosophical work, in a letter of defence addressed to the Duke of Würtemberg, Oetinger says, "Thirty years previously I had studied Swedenborg's *Principia Rerum Naturalium* in folio, which I preferred much to Wolff's philosophy, on account of its leading to the Sacred Scripture. It is wonderful how a philosopher, who was accustomed to think according to rules of mechanics, should have become a prophet."

We have now shown the esteem for Swedenborg of two of the men named by Kürtz as the leading religious spirits of this period in Germany — Jung-Stilling and Oetinger. That of a third, Lavater, is sufficiently shown in two letters to Swedenborg, the second and shorter of which we here copy : —

EMANUEL SWEDENBORG

"*Most noble, venerable, and beloved in Christ our Lord:*—I have taken the liberty of writing to you a second time, as it is likely you may not have received my other letter, on account of your travels; but I have at last learned by what means this will probably reach you.

"I revere the wonderful gifts you have received from God. I revere the wisdom which shines forth from your writings, and therefore cannot but seek the friendship of so great and excellent a man now living. If what is reported be true, God will show you how much I seek to converse with you in the simplicity of my mind. I am a young man, not yet thirty years old, a minister of the Gospel; I am and shall remain employed in the cause of Christ as long as I live. I have written something on the happiness of the future life. O, if I could exchange letters with you on this subject, or rather converse!

"I add some writing: you shall know my soul.

"One thing I beg of you, Divinely inspired man! I beseech you by the Lord not to refuse me!

"In the month of March, 1768, died Felix Hess, my best friend, a youth of Zürich, twenty-four years of age, an upright man, of a noble mind,

LATER PERIOD OF LIFE: CONCLUSION

striving after a Christian spirit, but not yet clothed with Christ. Tell me, I pray, what he is doing. Paint to me his figure, state, etc., in such words that I may know that God's truth is in you. . . .

"I am your brother in Christ. Answer very soon a sincere brother; and answer the letter I have sent in such a manner that *I may see* what I am believing on the testimony of others.

"Christ be with us, to whom we belong, living or dead.

"JOHN CASPER LAVATER,
"*Minister at the Orphan Asylum.*

"ZÜRICH IN SWITZERLAND
"Sept. 24, 1769."

Matthius Claudius, a third of Kürtz's five faithful sons of the Church, a poet and religious writer, had no personal acquaintance with Swedenborg, but reflected the esteem of others.

"Now," he says, "after Swedenborg had made himself acquainted with all the erudition of his time, and after the greatest honors had been bestowed upon him by individuals and whole societies, he began to see spirits. . . . He was always a virtuous man, and one who was interiorly affected with the beauty and majesty of the visible world. . . . We cannot help thinking that there are spirits, and Swedenborg often affirmed in his lifetime with great earnestness, and even on his death-bed . . . that he was able to see spirits, and had seen them. Now as the new world really existed long before Columbus found it out, though we in Europe were ignorant of its existence, so perhaps there may be a means to see spirits. . . . In the opinion of many wise people there lies a great deal of truth hidden perhaps close by us."

And Father Oberlin, of Ban-de-la-Roche, fourth of Kürtz's five most brilliant and best-known names of the faithful sons of the Church, held in reverence everywhere for his love and piety, was asked by an English visitor, the Rev. J. H. Smithson, whether he had read any of the works of Swedenborg.

"He immediately reached a book, and clapping his hand upon it, expressive of great satisfaction, told me that he had had this treasure a great many years in his library, and that he knew from his own experience that everything related in it was true. This treasure was Swedenborg's work on Heaven and Hell." In answer to inquiry how he came to this conviction, "he replied that

LATER PERIOD OF LIFE: CONCLUSION

when he first came to reside as pastor among the inhabitants of Steinthal, they had many superstitious notions respecting the proximity of the spiritual world, and of the appearance of various objects and phenomena in that world which from time to time were seen by some of the people belonging to his flock. For instance, it was not unusual for a person who had died to appear to some individual in the valley. This gift of second sight, or the opening of the spiritual sight, to see objects in a spiritual state of existence, was however confined to a few persons, and continued but a short period and at different intervals of time. The report of every new occurrence of this kind was brought to Oberlin, who at length became so much annoyed that he was resolved to put down this species of superstition, as he called it, from the pulpit, and exerted himself for a considerable time to this end, but with little or no desirable effect. Cases became more numerous, and the circumstances so striking as even to stagger the scepticism of Oberlin himself. About this time, being on a visit to Strasburg, he met with the work on Heaven and Hell, which a friend [probably Jung-

EMANUEL SWEDENBORG

world. . . . We cannot help thinking that there are spirits, and Swedenborg often affirmed in his lifetime with great earnestness, and even on his death-bed . . . that he was able to see spirits, and had seen them. Now as the new world really existed long before Columbus found it out, though we in Europe were ignorant of its existence, so perhaps there may be a means to see spirits. . . . In the opinion of many wise people there lies a great deal of truth hidden perhaps close by us."

And Father Oberlin, of Ban-de-la-Roche, fourth of Kürtz's five most brilliant and best-known names of the faithful sons of the Church, held in reverence everywhere for his love and piety, was asked by an English visitor, the Rev. J. H. Smithson, whether he had read any of the works of Swedenborg.

"He immediately reached a book, and clapping his hand upon it, expressive of great satisfaction, told me that he had had this treasure a great many years in his library, and that he knew from his own experience that everything related in it was true. This treasure was Swedenborg's work on Heaven and Hell." In answer to inquiry how he came to this conviction, " he replied that

LATER PERIOD OF LIFE: CONCLUSION

when he first came to reside as pastor among the inhabitants of Steinthal, they had many superstitious notions respecting the proximity of the spiritual world, and of the appearance of various objects and phenomena in that world which from time to time were seen by some of the people belonging to his flock. For instance, it was not unusual for a person who had died to appear to some individual in the valley. This gift of second sight, or the opening of the spiritual sight, to see objects in a spiritual state of existence, was however confined to a few persons, and continued but a short period and at different intervals of time. The report of every new occurrence of this kind was brought to Oberlin, who at length became so much annoyed that he was resolved to put down this species of superstition, as he called it, from the pulpit, and exerted himself for a considerable time to this end, but with little or no desirable effect. Cases became more numerous, and the circumstances so striking as even to stagger the scepticism of Oberlin himself. About this time, being on a visit to Strasburg, he met with the work on Heaven and Hell, which a friend [probably Jung-

EMANUEL SWEDENBORG

Stilling] recommended him to peruse. This work, as he informed me, gave him a full and satisfactory explanation of the extraordinary cases occurring in his valley, and which he himself was at length, from evidences which could not be doubted, constrained to admit. The satisfactory solution of these extraordinary cases afforded great pleasure to his mind, and he read the 'treasure,' as he called it, very attentively and with increasing delight. He no longer doubted the nearness of the spiritual world; yea, he believed that man by virtue of his better part — his immortal mind — is already an inhabitant of the spiritual world, in which after the death of the material body he is to continue his existence forever. He plainly saw, from the correspondent relation existing between the two worlds, that when it pleased the Lord, man might easily be placed by opening his spiritual senses in open communication with the world of spirits. This, he observed, was frequently the case with the seers mentioned in the Old Testament; and why might it not be so now, if the Divine providence saw fit, in order to instruct mankind more fully in respect to their relation to a spiritual state of

LATER PERIOD OF LIFE: CONCLUSION

existence, and to replenish their minds with more accurate and copious views respecting heaven, the final home of the good, and hell, the final abode of the wicked? . . . From seeing, as explained by Swedenborg, that the Lord's kingdom is a kingdom of uses, Oberlin resolved all the exertions and operations of his life into one element — USE. He taught his people that to be useful, and to shun all evil as sin against the Lord in being useful, is the truly heavenly life."

Carl Robsahm, who was intimate with Swedenborg in his later years, left memoirs of him, from which we take the following details: —

"Swedenborg's property [in Stockholm] was about a stone's cast in length and in breadth. The rooms of his dwelling-house were small and plain; but were comfortable for him, though scarcely for any one else. Although he was a learned man, no books were ever seen in his room except his Hebrew and Greek Bible, and his manuscript indexes to his own works, by which, in making quotations, he was saved the trouble of examining all that he had previously written or printed.

"Swedenborg worked without much regard to

the distinction of day and night, having no fixed time for labor or rest. 'When I am sleepy,' he said, 'I go to bed.' All the attendance he required from his servant, his gardener's wife, consisted in her making his bed and placing a large jug of water in his anteroom, his housekeeping being so arranged that he could make his own coffee in his study; and this coffee he drank in great abundance, both day and night, and with a great deal of sugar. When not invited out, his dinner consisted of nothing but a roll soaked in boiled milk; and this was his meal always when he dined at home. He never at that time used wine or strong drink, nor did he eat anything in the evening; but in company he would eat freely, and indulge moderately in a social glass.

"The fire in the stove of his study was never allowed to go out, from autumn through the whole of winter until spring; for as he always needed coffee, and as he always made it himself, without milk or cream, and as he had never any definite time for sleeping, he always required to have a fire.

"His sleeping-room was always without fire; and when he lay down, according to the severity

LATER PERIOD OF LIFE: CONCLUSION

of the winter, he covered himself with three or four woollen blankets. But I remember one winter which was so cold that he was obliged to move his bed into his study.

"As soon as he awoke, he went into his study, where he always found glowing embers, put wood on the burning coals and a few pieces of birch bark — which for convenience he used to purchase in bundles so as to be able to make a fire quickly — and then he sat down to write.

"In his drawing-room was the marble table which he afterward presented to the Royal College of Mines; this room was neat and genteel, but plain.

"His dress in winter consisted of a fur coat of reindeer skin, and in summer of a dressing-gown; both well worn, as became a philosopher's wardrobe. His wearing apparel was simple, but neat. Yet it happened sometimes that when he prepared to go out, and his people did not call attention to it, something would be forgotten or neglected in his dress; so that, for instance, he would put one buckle of gems and another of silver in his shoes — an instance of which absence of mind I myself saw at my father's house, where he was invited to dine, and the occurrence greatly amused several young girls, who took occasion to laugh at the old gentleman.

"It was difficult for him to talk quickly, for he then stammered, especially when he was obliged to talk in a foreign tongue. Of foreign languages, in addition to the learned languages, he understood well French, English, Dutch, German, and Italian; for he had journeyed several times in these countries. He spoke slowly, and it was always a pleasure to be with him at table, for whenever Swedenborg spoke, all other talk was hushed; and the slowness with which he spoke had the effect of restraining the frivolous remarks of the curious in the assembly. At first he used to talk freely about his visions and his explanations of Scripture; but when this displeased the clergy, and they pronounced him a heretic or a downright madman, he resolved to be more sparing of his communications in company, or at all events to be more on his guard, so as not to offer an opportunity to scoffers of inveighing against what they could not understand as well as himself.

"I once addressed the pastor of our parish, an old and esteemed clergyman, and asked him what

LATER PERIOD OF LIFE: CONCLUSION

I ought to think of Swedenborg's visions and of his explanations of the Bible. This honorable man answered me with the spirit of true tolerance: 'Let God be the judge how these things are in reality! But I cannot pass the same judgment upon him that many others do; I have spoken with him myself, and I have found in company where he was with me that he is a pious and good man.'

"The chaplain of the Imperial Russian Legation, Oronoskow, who was in Stockholm during the time of the ambassador, Count Ostermann, was a monk of the Alexander-Newsky order, and led an orderly and pious life — quite differently from the other Russian priests who had been here before him. He became acquainted with me and I lent him Swedenborg's books, which he said he read with the greatest delight. He desired to see Swedenborg and to talk with this remarkable man. I complied with his desire, and invited Swedenborg and him to dinner, in company with the late President of the Royal College of Commerce, Mr. von Carleson, and the Councillor of Chancery, Mr. Berch, together with several of my relatives. During dinner the chaplain asked Swedenborg, among other things, whether he had seen the Empress Elizabeth. Swedenborg answered, 'I have seen her often, and I know that she is in a very happy state.' This answer brought tears of joy into the chaplain's eyes, who said that she had been good and just. 'Yes,' said Swedenborg, 'her kind feeling for her people was made known after her death in the other life; for there it was shown that she never went into council without praying to God and asking for His counsel and assistance, in order that she might govern well her country and her people.' This gladdened the chaplain so much that he expressed his joyful surprise by silence and tears. . . .

"When he [Swedenborg] left Sweden for the last time, he came of his own accord to me at the bank on the day he was to leave, and gave me a protest against any condemnation of his writings during his absence; which protest was based on the law of Sweden, and in which he stated that the House of the Clergy was not the only judge in matters of religion, inasmuch as theology belonged also to the other Houses. On this occasion I asked him the same question as before, namely, whether I should ever see him again. His answer

LATER PERIOD OF LIFE: CONCLUSION

was tender and touching:—'Whether I shall come again, that,' said he, 'I do not know; but of this I can assure you, for the Lord has promised to me, that I shall not die until I have received from the press this work, the *Vera Christiana Religio*, which is now ready to be printed, and for the sake of which I now undertake this journey; but if we do not meet again in the body, we shall meet in the presence of the Lord, provided we live in this world according to His will, and not according to our own.' He then took leave of me in as blithe and cheerful a frame of mind as if he had been a man in his best of years; and the same day he departed from Sweden for the last time.

"I asked Swedenborg once whether his explanations would be received in Christendom. 'About that,' said he, 'I can say nothing; but I suppose that in their proper time they will be received, for otherwise the Lord would not have disclosed what has heretofore lain concealed.'

"He was never ill, except when temptations came over him, but he was frequently troubled with toothache. I came to him once on such an occasion, when he complained of a severe toothache, which had continued for several days. I recommended a common remedy for soothing the pain; but he answered at once that his toothache was not caused by a diseased nerve, but by the influx of hell from hypocrites who tempted him, and who by correspondence caused this pain which, he said, he knew would soon cease and leave him.

"Respecting his temptations, I collected information from his modest servants, the old gardener and his wife, who told me with sympathizing and compassionate words that Swedenborg often spoke aloud in his room, and was indignant when evil spirits were with him. This they could hear the more distinctly because their room was near his. When he was asked why he had been so restless during the night, he answered that permission had been given to evil spirits to revile him, and that he spoke to and was indignant with them. It often happened that he wept bitterly, and called out with a loud voice, and prayed to the Lord that He would not leave him in the temptation which had come upon him. The words which he cried out were these: 'O Lord, help me! O Lord my God, do not forsake me!' When it was all over, and his people asked him about

LATER PERIOD OF LIFE: CONCLUSION

the cause of his lamentation, he said, 'God be praised! it is over now. You must not trouble yourselves about me; for whatever happens to me is permitted by the Lord, and He does not suffer me to be tempted more than He sees that I can bear.'

"Once it was very remarkable that after such a lamentation he lay down and did not rise from his bed for several days and nights. This caused his people much uneasiness; they talked with one another and supposed that he had died from some great fright. They thought of having the door forced open, or of calling in his intimate friends. At last the man went to the window, and to his great joy saw that his master was still alive, for he turned himself in bed. The next day he rang the bell, and then the housekeeper went in and told him of her own and her husband's uneasiness at his condition; whereupon he said with a cheerful countenance that he was doing well, and that he did not need anything. She was satisfied with this answer, for neither of his servants dared to interrogate him, since they had the same opinion of him as the old clergyman in my parish; and they added that such a wise and learned man would never distress himself with work and temptations if he did not know whence they came."

At another time Robsahm quotes the gardener's wife as saying —

"'I can see when he has spoken with heavenly spirits, for his face has then an expression of gentleness, cheerfulness, and contentment which is charming; but after he has conversed with evil spirits, he looks sad.' . .

"During the session of the Diet he was interested in hearing news from the House of Nobles, of which he was a member by virtue of his being the head of the Swedenborg family. He wrote several memorials; but when he saw that party-spirit and self-interest struggled for mastery, he went rarely to the House of Nobles. In his conversations with his friends he inveighed against the spirit of dissension among the members of the Diet; and in acting with a party he was never a party man, but loved truth and honesty in all that he did.

"I asked Swedenborg whether in our times it was worth while to pay attention to dreams; upon which he answered that the Lord no longer at the present day makes revelations by dreams;

LATER PERIOD OF LIFE : CONCLUSION

but that nevertheless it may happen that one who understands correspondences may derive advantage from his dreams — just as a person that is awake may examine his own state by comparing his own will with God's commandments. . . .

"Whatever Swedenborg wrote was printed from his own manuscript, and he never needed the help of an amanuensis. His handwriting was difficult to read when he became older; but he said to me, 'The Dutch printers read my handwriting as easily as the English do.' There is one thing to be observed with regard to most of his spiritual writings, that the proof-sheets were corrected very badly, so that errata occur very often; the cause of this, he said, was that the printer had undertaken the proof-reading, as well as the printing.

"As Swedenborg in his younger days did not think of the work which was to occupy him in his more advanced years, it can easily be imagined that in his time he was not only a learned man, but also a polished gentleman; for a man of such extensive learning, who by his books, his travels, and his knowledge of languages had acquired distinction both at home and abroad, could not fail

EMANUEL SWEDENBORG

to possess the manners and everything else which in those so-called serious or sober times caused a man to be honored and made him agreeable in society. He was accordingly, even in his old age, cheerful, sprightly, and agreeable in company; yet at the same time his countenance presented those uncommon features which are seen only in men of great genius."

Robsahm's vivid picture of his friend may be supplemented by the slighter sketches of some of Swedenborg's visitors, with less intimate acquaintance. The royal librarian in Stockholm, Gjörwell, called on him in 1764 to request for the Royal Library a copy of the works he had lately published. His account of his visit to Swedenborg is simple, and pleasant to read:—

"I met him in the garden adjoining his house in the Södermalm [southern part of Stockholm], where he was engaged in tending his plants, attired in a simple garment. The house in which he lives is of wood; it is low and looks like a garden-house; its windows also are in the direction of the garden. Without knowing me or the nature of my errand, he said, smiling, 'Perhaps you would like to take a walk in the garden.' I an-

LATER PERIOD OF LIFE: CONCLUSION

swered that I wished to have the honor of calling upon him and asking him, on behalf of the Royal Library, for his latest works, so that we might have a complete set, especially as we had the former parts he had left with Wilde, the royal secretary. 'Most willingly,' he answered; 'besides, I had intended to send them there, as my purpose in publishing them has been to make them known and to place them in the hands of intelligent people.' I thanked him for his kindness, whereupon he showed them to me and took a walk with me in the garden.

"Although he is an old man and gray hair protruded in every direction from under his wig, he walked briskly, was fond of talking, and spoke with a certain cheerfulness. His countenance was indeed thin and meagre, but cheerful and smiling. By and by he began of his own accord to speak of his views; and as it had been in reality my second purpose to hear them with my own ears, I listened to him with eager attention, not challenging any of his statements, but simply asking him questions, as if for my own enlightenment."

The substance of his statements, and of what

EMANUEL SWEDENBORG

I drew from him by polite questions, consists mainly in what follows:—

"His doctrinal system of theology, which he in common with other Christians bases upon our common Revelation, the Sacred Scripture, consists principally in this — that faith alone is a pernicious doctrine, and that good works are the proper means for becoming better in time, and for leading a blessed life in eternity. That in order to acquire the ability or power to do good works, prayer to the Only God is required, and that man also must labor with himself, because God does not use compulsion with us nor does He work any miracles for our conversion. As regards the rest, man must live in his appointed place, acquiring the same learning, and leading a life similar to that of other honest and modest persons who live temperately and piously."

The Rev. Nicholas Collin, in 1820 rector of the quaint old Swedish church in Philadelphia — the same that was built in 1700 under Bishop Swedberg's charge — lived when a young man three years in Stockholm, at a time when "Swedenborg was a great object of public attention in that metropolis, and his extraordinary character was a fre-

LATER PERIOD OF LIFE: CONCLUSION

quent topic of discussion. Not seldom he appeared in public and mixed in private circles; therefore sufficient opportunities were given to make observations on him." Mr. Collin was not a follower of Swedenborg, but obligingly gave public information about him on several occasions. Of a visit of his own, he writes as follows:—

"In the summer of 1766 I waited on him at his house, introducing myself, with an apology for the freedom I took, assuring him that it was not in the least from youthful presumption (I was then twenty), but from a strong desire of conversing with a character so celebrated. He received me very kindly. It being early in the afternoon, delicate coffee, without eatables, was served, agreeably to the Swedish custom: he was also, like pensive men in general, fond of this beverage. We conversed for nearly three hours, principally on the nature of human souls and their states in the invisible world, discussing the principal theories of psychology by various authors — among them the celebrated Dr. Wallerius, late professor of Natural Theology at Upsal. He asserted positively, as he often does in his works, that he had intercourse with spirits of deceased persons. I presumed therefore to request of him, as a great favor, to procure me an interview with my brother, who had departed this life a few months before, a young clergyman officiating in Stockholm and esteemed for his devotion, erudition, and virtue. He answered that, God having for wise and good purposes separated the world of spirits from ours, a communication is never granted without cogent reasons, and asked what my motives were. I confessed that I had none besides gratifying brotherly affection and an ardent wish to explore scenes so sublime and interesting to a serious mind. He replied that my motives were good, but not sufficient; that if any important spiritual or temporal concern of mine had been the case, he would then have solicited permission from those angels who regulate such matters."

In another letter Mr. Collin said —

"Swedenborg was universally esteemed for his various erudition in mathematics, mineralogy, etc., and for his probity, benevolence, and general virtue. Being very old when I saw him, he was thin and pale; but he still retained traces of beauty in his physiognomy, and a dignity in his tall and erect stature."

LATER PERIOD OF LIFE: CONCLUSION

And to a good friend of ours Mr. Collin said —

"Swedenborg was of a stature a little above the common size, of very perfect form, erect and easy in his carriage, with a placid expression of dignity beaming from his countenance; he was affable in his manners, easy of access, and always ready to converse freely on subjects relating to either world, but singularly unapt to obtrude his ideas on others, either in conversation or by his writings, though firm and unwavering with regard to the truth of his relations. His history from very early life was reputed to be such as evinced great purity, as well as strength, of mental character." Speaking of the affair of the Queen of Sweden, which her librarian had told him from her mouth, and of other similar occurrences, Mr. Collin said that he believed "no one at Stockholm presumed to doubt of his having some kind of supernatural intercourse with the spiritual world in all these cases," and this, he said, was not strange, "for at that time occasional communication between this and the invisible world was believed to exist by many of the most learned men in Sweden."

We have seen that at his home in Stockholm — a simple one-story house in his loved garden —

EMANUEL SWEDENBORG

Swedenborg was cared for in later life by his gardener and wife. Of these good friends this pleasant story is told by one who paid them a visit after their employer's decease. As they themselves told him —

"One day the old man and the old woman, the modest gardener-folks [who had been disturbed by meddling neighbors] dressed in their holiday suits, entered Swedenborg's silent study, the room with the brown panel-paintings, the gable windows, and a view out on the lilac bushes.

"Swedenborg sat with his head resting upon both hands, poring over a large book. Surprised by the unusual noise, he raised his head and looked toward the door. There stood the good gardener-folks, though but the middle of the week, both dressed in their holiday clothes, bowing and curtseying. On Swedenborg's grave but cheerful countenance, there played an inquiring smile.

"'Why dressed up so, Andersson and Margaret?' he said. 'What do you want?'

"This was not in truth easy to say, and, instead of an answer, Margaret began to cry, and her husband crushed his hat into a thousand wrinkles, and

LATER PERIOD OF LIFE: CONCLUSION

in his heart wished himself more than a thousand miles away.

"'Is there any care that lies upon your hearts, any distress which has suddenly come over you?' said Swedenborg — 'then speak out plainly, and, with God's help, it will all go well again.'

"'Yes,' at last said the old gardener, 'yes, we wish to leave the Assessor's service.'"

"Swedenborg seemed surprised. 'Leave me! and why?' he asked, with his penetrating, friendly look, which pierced them to their very heart; 'I thought, as we were growing old together, we should to our very end remain faithful to one another, and never separate in this life.'

"'Yes, so also we thought ourselves,' burst out the housewife, almost overcome with tears; 'for thirty years we have served you, and I thought it would be God's pleasure that we should die in your garden, and under your eyes; but, but —'

"'Speak out, woman; what lies so heavily upon your heart? I know that both of you think a great deal of me. Is it not so?'

"'Yes, before God it is so,' said both of them together.

"'Speak out then,' said Swedenborg, with a

smile, 'and then we may be able to help the matter.'

"The housewife, whose strong emotion gave her courage to speak, and words to express her thoughts, at last began: — 'Yes, people say we ought not to serve you any longer, because you are not a right Christian.'

"'Nothing else, my good woman,' said Swedenborg quietly; 'nothing else? Well, let the world judge so; but why should you think so?'

"'You see you never go to church; for years you have never been inside of St. Mary's church.'

"'Have you never read,' replied Swedenborg solemnly, 'that, where two or three are gathered together in the Lord's name, there is His church and meeting-place? Do you believe that it is the steeple and copper roof which makes a holy place of it? Do you believe that it is holy for any one else but him who has in his heart Christ's church? Do you believe that it is the walls, organ, and pulpit, which constitute its holiness?'

"'No, no; I know that well enough.'

"'Well, then, here at home, in this room, in the arbor, in the garden, wherever a man or spirit lives within or without space and time,

LATER PERIOD OF LIFE : CONCLUSION

wherever a prayer is either thought or read, wherever a voice of thanksgiving is sent up to Him who is the Giver of all good, there is His church; and it is consequently here where I live sheltered from the world.'

"Both the faithful servants bowed their heads and said — 'But this is not the way of the world.'

"'The way of the world, my friends?' replied Swedenborg, 'I suppose the way of the world is Christian, is it not?'

"'Yes, it is.'

"'In name it is, but not in spirit and in truth. Faith without works is a dead faith: a flower which does not live is nothing but lifeless dust; and faith which does not live in every action of man is a dead faith — it is no faith at all. Here, my friends, see what this Christian world really does. They call indeed upon Him, the only Son, in their times of need, but they forget both His teaching and His life. Like an obstinate child who despises warning, they rush into all manner of lusts, into pride and wickedness, which are like a thin, frail covering over an abyss; and over this yawning abyss they scoff at their Teacher, and act foolishly and madly until this covering breaks. Then they call out for help, but in vain, for they have long since forfeited it; sometimes they are dragged up again, but in their foolish pride they let go the Saving Hand, they spurn the healing repentance, and continue their course of vain talk and idle sport. So does the Christian world, and they think that all that is necessary for them is to have a priest to speak to them a few hours in the week about God and the Saviour; and they do not think that any more is required of them than to hear and to forget. They therefore believe that it is outward gesture, the singing of psalms, and the tones of the organ, together with the empty sound of recited prayers, which penetrate to the Lord in heaven. Truly when the people prostrate themselves in the churches, then it is the voice of a few only that penetrates to the Lord.

"'Let me tell you something. To-day there was a little child sitting in the street, a little blind girl, who folded her little hands upon her lap, and turned her darkened eyes towards heaven; and when I saw her, and asked her, "What makes you look so happy, although you

LATER PERIOD OF LIFE : CONCLUSION

are blind?"—the little girl said, "I am thinking of God, our Father, who will some day take me to Him, and show me all His splendor." Truly, my good people, it was only at the corner of the street that she sat, yet I took off my hat, and bowed my head, for I knew that God was near, and that this was a holy place. . . . And now, my friends, look back upon these thirty years during which you have followed me almost daily with your eyes, and then judge whether it is I or others who are Christian. Judge for yourselves — I submit myself to your judgment — and then do what you deem to be right.'

"He beckoned with his hand and they went away; and then quietly, as if nothing had happened, he continued his reading.

"The next day they stood again, in their week-day clothes, in the presence of their master, who asked them with a friendly smile — 'Well, how did the examination turn out?'

"'**Oh**, master Assessor,' said both of them, 'we looked for a single word, for a single action, which was not in agreement with what the Lord had commanded us, yet we could not find a single one.'

"'Very well,' said Swedenborg; 'but it is **not**

quite so; many thoughts have been, and many an action has been, not perfectly straight; yet I have tried to do as well as I could. And as a child, who in the beginning spells out his words, and stumbles often before he can read, provided he goes to work lovingly and cheerfully and strives hard to do better, is loved by his father, so also it may have been with me; at least I pray and hope that it may be so. But you will remain with me?'

"'Yes, master Assessor, until our death.'

"'Thank you, my friends; I knew it would be so. Let people say what they please about my teachings, but do you judge them by my life: if they agree, then all is right; but if there is the least disagreement between them, then one of the two must be wrong.'

"When the little old woman had finished her story, which she had told after the manner of her people, by constantly repeating 'said the Assessor,' and 'said I,' her eyes were glistening with emotion, and she added — 'God, indeed, must have forsaken us when He allowed us to go astray so far as to suspect our own Assessor of not being a Christian.'

LATER PERIOD OF LIFE: CONCLUSION

"The good old woman took us through the garden, which was decked in its greatest autumnal splendor, and was loaded with berries and fruits; and as we were walking along, with a side glance at me, she said that the Assessor never allowed children in his garden; 'but sometimes,' she added, 'he lets one or the other slip in, but not before he has looked at him and has said — "Let the child pass, he will not take anything without leave," and he has never made a mistake. This he sees from their eyes.'"[1]

It was in London that Swedenborg's last days were passed, in the house of Richard Shearsmith, a respectable wig-maker, with whom he had lived two years during a previous stay in that city. He liked this quiet home because he found peace and harmony there, while, according to Mr. Shearsmith, his lodger was "a blessing to the house, for they had harmony and good business while he was with them." He added that "to a good man, like Swedenborg, every day of his life is a Sabbath," and that "to the last day of his life he always conducted himself in the most rational, prudent, pious, and Christian-like man-

[1] *Altartaflan*, by Dr. Wetterbergh.

ner." Being then at the close of his eighty-fourth year, near Christmas, Swedenborg had a paralytic stroke that deprived him of speech and caused him to lie in a lethargic state for more than three weeks, in which he took no other nourishment than a little tea or cold water from time to time. By the last of February he told Mrs. Shearsmith what day would be his last, and with "a sound mind, memory, and understanding" to his last hour, on Sunday evening, March 29, 1772, about five o'clock, pleased to find the hour had come, this Sunday child thanked his friends, asked God to bless them, and with a gentle sigh yielded his last breath. Friendly Swedes in London took charge of the last services, at which their pastor, Arvid Ferelius, officiated, and the body was deposited in the vault of the Swedish Ulrica-Eleonora church. In this little church which had often welcomed Swedenborg as a worshipper, his remains reposed until the building itself was no longer required in its location and was to be taken down. Then at the request of the Royal Swedish Academy of Sciences the Swedish Government, having obtained permission of the English Government,

LATER PERIOD OF LIFE : CONCLUSION

in April, 1908, transported these remains in a Swedish frigate to their native land. There by vote of the Swedish Parliament they are to have their final resting-place in a suitable sarcophagus in a chapel of the cathedral at Upsal, near their early home. The general interest exerted by this public restoration in Europe and America, with the gratification of the Swedish people at the honors bestowed on their illustrious compatriot, may be mainly due to his increasing celebrity as a scientist and philosopher. But those who accept Swedenborg as their Divinely appointed teacher recognize in it an extending preparation in the world for his acceptance in that capacity.

Do we ask for a sign of the truth of Swedenborg's mission as the Divinely appointed interpreter of the Holy Scriptures, and as the harbinger of the new age of the Lord's Church, even that foreseen in vision by John as the Holy City descending from God out of heaven? The sign of this second coming of our Lord was to be the clear vision of the Son of Man in the clouds of heaven — that is, in the clouds of obscurity through which men looked toward the Sun of heaven — clouds drawn from the ill-understood and misinterpreted letter of the Word. The proof of Swedenborg's mission will be found in the fulfilment of this sign — to each one in the clearer vision that by the interpretation of Swedenborg he now obtains of the Lord of heaven throughout His Holy Word. This sign no one can see for another, but every one must see for himself, and in very truth only by the aid of the Holy Spirit. But though this special enlightenment is to be found in the interpretations of Swedenborg as nowhere else, the coming of the Son of Man was to be as the light that shineth out of the east even unto the west. And while none but students of Swedenborg's writings can recognize in him the harbinger, the Christian world perceives that new light is being diffused. The historians point to the middle of the eighteenth century as the date of the breaking of the light. Soon after that date apprehension of the impending judgment began to subside. The Church began to feel new life. As century after century the time for judgment is left behind and the new life of the Church becomes better established, more and more generally will be recognized the truth of Sweden-

LATER PERIOD OF LIFE: CONCLUSION

borg's description of the spiritual accomplishment of the judgment, and of its effect in dissipating the clouds of heaven.

In deducing from the Word under guidance of the Holy Spirit the doctrines of the New Jerusalem, the tabernacle of God among men, Swedenborg contemplated no new outward church organization. He describes orderly church government, but in no new form. His expectation seems to have been that the light of the new heaven, such as had been revealed to him, would gradually permeate the whole Christian Church and regenerate it. Such is the expectation of all who are so happy as to be familiar with his theological works. But naturally those who accept these doctrines as Divinely revealed through Swedenborg, unless specially attached to some existing church, believe it most suitable and most useful to organize together as a distinct body. This they have done first in England, then in America, and in smaller numbers in various parts of the world, under the title of the New Church, the New-Jerusalem Church, or the Church of the New Jerusalem — known more generally as Swedenborgians. In England the

EMANUEL SWEDENBORG

several congregations unite in a General Conference, embracing between six and seven thousand members. In America the principal larger organization is called the General Convention, of nearly the same membership.

Little effort is made by these several bodies to increase their numbers, none to induce any to leave the churches to which they belong. But efforts are continually made to keep the theological works of Swedenborg in abundant supply and within the reach of all who care to learn from him the True Christian Religion, as set forth in his last great work, under that title.

INDEX

INDEX

Figures refer to pages.

Abbey and Overton, quoted, 15.
Adam and Eve, the Most Ancient Church, 5, 6.
Anatomy, studies in, 92.
Atheism in 18th century, 14.

Baglivius, referred to, 66.
Barnard, Sir John, quoted, 15.
Behm, Sara, 25.
Belgium, visited, 76.
Bengel, quoted, 14.
Benzelius, Ericus, Archbishop, 26, 48, 56–73, 92.
Benzelius, Ericus, the younger, 38, 45, 58, 63.
Bishops, friendly and otherwise, 218, 228, 237.
Brain, study of, 113, 125–128.
Brunswick, Duke of, 76.

Canaan, perhaps home of Most Ancient Church, 8.
Canal, between North and Baltic seas, 58, 61, 62.
Candlesticks, representation of, 192.
Carlyle, quoted, 16.
Censor of books, 67.
Change of heart, necessary, 24.
Charity, come again, 20.
Charles XI, friendly to Swedberg, 24.
Charles XII, appointed Swedberg bishop, 25; returned to Sweden and employed Polheimer and Swedenborg, 51; appointed Swedenborg Assessor, 51, 54; interested in Dædalus, 57, 62; in salt works, 57; in canal, 58, 61.
Christianity, regarded as mere prejudice of infant race, 16.
Church, Most Ancient, represented by Adam, 6. Ancient, 6–8. Hebrew, 9, 10. Christian, new age, 1, 283–285; error of first age, 12–18. Reformed, error, 13, 14. New, of whom formed, 195; when to come, 227, 228, 285; organization, 285, 286.
City of God, the end of creation, 115, 116, 123, 131, 132.
Claudius, Matthius, quoted, 253, 254.
Coleridge, quoted, 117.
College of Mines, Swedenborg appointed to, 51, 52; composition, 55; records, 55; duties, 56, 90.
Collin, quoted, 270–273.
Consummation of the Age, chapter 1.
Creation, its order that of spiritual development, 5.
Creator, highest conception of, 2; man in His image, 2; knowledge of is supreme end in view, 29, 70, 93, 94–105, 122, 131.
Cuno, quoted, 230–237.

Dædalus, 46, 50–53, 56–62, 65.
Deism, in 18th century, 14.
Descartes, 60, 61.

INDEX

Diet, Swedish, 68, 79–84, 211–217, 266.
Disciples, of the Lord, looked for reward, 12.
Doctrine, to be drawn from the Scriptures, 142.
Dörner, quoted, 15.
Dreams, no revelation by, 266.
Dumas, quoted, 79.

Elfvius, Professor, 43, 50.
Elizabeth, Empress of Russia, 262.
Emerentia Polhem, 63, 64.
England, visited, 31, 162.
Enlightenment, from love of truth for truth's sake, 141–143.
Esberg, nephew of Benzelius, 62.

Faith, above all demonstration and most happy, 119, 158–161; faith alone, doctrine of, 195–199; this doctrine pernicious, 270; of new heaven and new church, 204.
Fire, in Stockholm, 244–246.
Fires of hell, remorses of conscience? 70.
France, condition in 18th century, 16; visited, 38, 92.
Frederic, King, 91.

Garden, Swedenborg's, 210, 217, 281.
Gardener and wife, 274–281.
Genesis, spiritual content of first chapter, 4.
Gentiles, receive the light, 10, 11.
Germany, condition of in 18th century, 16; visited, 76.
Gjörwell, quoted, 268.

Gospel, first accepted through hope or fear, 12; preached anew in world of spirits, 200.

Halley, consulted, 35, 36.
Heaven, speculations about, 132–134; the new, of whom formed, 193, 194, 201.
Hebrew, nation and language prophetic, 9; maternal service for Christianity, 10.
Holland, visited, 38, 76.
Holy Spirit, the second coming with, 1, 191; experience with, 145–147, 169.
Holy Supper, attendance at, 147, 163.
Höpken, favored by Swedenborg, 215; quoted, 219–224.

Infinite, The, argument for, 95–105.
Isaksson, Daniel, 23.
Italy, visited, 93.

John, representing the love of the Church, 19, 191; his vision, 20, 192.
Judgment, of the Christian Church, 17–20; in the world of spirits, 21, 193; Swedenborg's part in, 200; effect of, 200.
Jung-Stilling, quoted, 237–243.

Kant, his results, 93, 94; quoted, 244–248.

Lavater, quoted, 251, 252.
Lecker, Archbishop, quoted, 16.
Leibnitz, quoted, 15.
Lewis, publisher, quoted, 209.

INDEX

Lord Jesus Christ, predictions of second coming, 1, 20; in Him first seen man in image of God, 11; first did the will of the Father on earth, 11; seen by disciples in glory, 18; His coming needed for conjunction of man with God, 100–105; and for the Head of human society, 133, 134; how He now shows Himself, 171, 186; His first coming the beginning of permanent dwelling with men, 189; distinction between the human and the Divine in Him, 206–208.

Luther, revolt against the Roman church, 13; his error, 13, 14.

Man, primeval, little known, 5.
Metals, study of, 73, 74, 79, 89; recommendations to Diet about, 83, 84.
Muses, referred to, 50.

Nathorst, Professor, quoted, 68.
Newburger, quoted, 128.
Nexus, need of, the Son of God, 100–105.

Oberlin, Father, quoted, 254–257.
Oetinger, letter to, 141; quoted, 249–251.

Peter, representing the faith of the Church, 19.
Philosophy, elemental, 60, 61, 66, 77–79, 86–88, 90; spiritual, 95–105.

Pierce, Professor, quoted, 135.
Polheimer, 44, 49, 51, 54, 56.
Proofs, printer's, not well corrected, 267.
Purpose, the Divine, mirrored in the universe, 2; revealed in Scripture, 3; is man in the image of his Creator, 5.

Reason, relation to Revelation, 105; use and enjoyment of the faculty, 108–112, 121; impaired by self-love, 110–112, 120.
Receipt, lost and found, 246–248.
Regeneration, nature of, 137–175; need of the world to learn, 150; deep, of Swedenborg, 173–175.
Representations, and correspondences, 124, 125.
Retzius, quoted, 129.
Roberg, Dr., 53, 61.
Robsahm, quoted, 170–172, 257–268.
Rules of life, 137, 138.
Russia, war with opposed by Swedenborg, 211.
Russians, approach of, 45.

Sacred Scripture, reveals the Divine will in man's thought and speech, 3, 22; a ladder of ascent into the Divine presence, 3; inwardly full of Divine wisdom, 3, 22; to be interpreted rationally by aid of the Holy Spirit, 22; philosophy can never be contrary to, 95; the only resort when reason fails, 105; belief in most happy, 119; unsealing of, 175–188, 192;

INDEX

everything in it has reference to the Lord, 178, 179; became flesh, 190; light now seen therein, 284.
Saint Paul's church finished, 32.
Salt works, 57.
Sandel's eulogy, 64.
Schlegel, quoted, 8, 9.
Series and Degrees, 113, 115.
Shearsmith, Richard, Swedenborg's stay in his family, 281, 282.
Ships, carried overland, 64.
Son of Man, sign of, 18, 106, 283, 284.
Spirits, presence perceived first without sight, 144; first spoken with, 170.
Springer, quoted, 226.
Spurgin, quoted, 117.
Stiernhjelm, referred to, 50.
Sun of Heaven, darkened, 14, 17; Divine presence in, 70; God the Sun of wisdom, 120; dependence on its light, 137; the Divine face to be seen in, 152.
Sunday child, Jesper Swedberg and family, 27.
Swedberg, Anna, 26, 31, 32, 44, 53.
Swedberg, Hedwig, 38.
Swedberg, Jesper, 23-26; at Upsal, 24, 25; Brunsbo, 25; revised Swedish Bible, 24; age, preaching, marriage, 25; family ennobled, 27, 68; author and in charge of missions, 27, 28; sense of heavenly protection, 28, 29; death, 91.
Swedenborg, Emanuel, parentage, 23; childhood, 24, 29; birth and name, 26; education, 30; plans of life, 30 *et seq.*; learns book-binding and music, 31; travels, 31, 75, 76, 85, 90, 92, 93, 209, 210, 228; studies Newton, 31, 32; visits Flamsteed, 32; love for his family and home, 32; immoderate desire for study, 33; learns trades, 33, 40; makes globes, 33, 34; his method for determining longitude, 34-36, 48, 49, 77; new methods in astronomy, 34; study of English poets, 35, 43, 44; lacks money abroad, 35; consults Halley, 35; study and practice of poetry, 36, 220; mathematical ambition, 36, 38, 40, goes to France, 37, 92; describes microscope and clock, 37, 38; visits distinguished men, 39; inventions, 41-43, 46, 47; interest in Polheimer's, 44, 49; wants to form a Society for Learning and Science, 44; seeks employment from Government, 46; writes letters in French, 48; appointed Assessor, 51-54, 75, 85; assists Polheimer, 54, 56; declines professorship of astronomy, 59; early essays, 59, 60, 65; tires of working for nothing, 70-72; plans in 1718, 71-73; betrothed to daughter of Polheimer, 63, 64; transports ships overland, 64, 220, writes on tremulations, 66; agrees with Baglivius, 66; geological studies, 67; first signature as "Swedenborg,"

INDEX

67, 68; seat in Diet, 68; studies in metallurgy, 73, 74, 79, 88, 89; salary as Assessor, 75, 85, 91; favored by Duke of Brunswick, 76; addresses to the Diet, 79–84, 211–217, 266; magnetic theory, 90; attendance at College of Mines, 55, 56, 79, 85, 90–92; studies anatomy, 92; uses experiments of others in preference to his own, 107, 108; discoveries, 128–130; faculty of reflection, 108; rules of life, 138; spiritual experience, 137–175; knew only later what he was being prepared for, 140, 141, 160, 162, 172; enlightened by love of truth for truth's sake, 143; instructed by dreams, 143–166; perceives presence of spirits but without seeing them, 144; temptations, 146–166, 264, 265; learned to be led not by spirits or angels, but by the Lord alone, 149, 187; was a mild Lutheran, 150, found himself most unworthy, 152, 163; new motto — I am Thine and not mine, 157; fainting fit, 167; appeared to write a fine hand, 167; habit of abstraction, 168, tacit respiration, 168; knew nothing at first of spirits, 168, 169; learned about different kinds, 169; first spoke with them, 170; warned against over-eating, 171; told what his work was to be, 172; deep regeneration, 173; full preparation for his work, 175, 186; in open company with spirits and angels many years, 180; suffering from spirits, 196; first affixes his name to theological works, 203; manner of later life, 209–248; food, 227, 258; gave receipts from Arcana to propagation of the Gospel, 210; opposed war with Russia, making of whiskey, and Bank loans on other than real estate, 211; defended the Government, 212–214; favored alliance with France, 215; was of the constitutional party, 215–217; fond of his garden and of children, 217, 223; on friendly terms with royal family, bishops, and all men of standing, 218; authority on finance, 220; predicts his arrival, 228; knew Springer's secret affairs, 229; society manners, 234, 267; learns subject of talk with deceased friend, 240; learns death of Emperor Peter, 111, 242; tells of fire in Stockholm, 244–246; where to find lost receipt, 246–248; understood French, English, Dutch, German, and Italian, 260; protested against judgment of his books by House of the clergy; handwriting, 267; declined to obtain interview without sufficient reason, 272; appearance, 272, 273; his communication with other world easily believed at Stockholm, 273; talk with gardener and wife, 274–280;

INDEX

tells of little blind girl, 278, 279; predicts time of death as it proved, 282; burial, recent removal of remains, 282, 283.

Trinity, error concerning, 14.
Tuxen, quoted, 219.

Ulrica Eleonora, 68.
Ulrica, Queen Louisa, 224–226.

Wilkinson, J. J. G., quoted, 77.
Wolf, Christopher, letter from, 92.
Works of Swedenborg,
  Scientific:— Principles of Chemistry, 77; Miscellaneous Observations, 77; Philosophical and Mineral Works, 85–90, 94, 251; Economy of the Animal Kingdom, 93, 106–118; Infinite and Final Cause of Creation, 95; Rational Psychology, 113, 130; Animal Kingdom, 118–132, 162, 163, 167; Worship and Love of God, 166, 172.
  Theological:— Heavenly Arcana, 177–188, 209, 210; Spiritual Diary, 144 *et seq.;* Apocalypse Explained, 193–208; Final Judgment, 194, 202; Heaven and Hell, 194; Earths in the Universe, 194; The New Jerusalem and its Heavenly Doctrine, 194; Apocalypse Revealed, 194, 202; Doctrines of the Lord, Sacred Scripture, Life, and Faith, 202; Divine Love and Wisdom, Divine Providence, Marriage Love, 202; Summary Exposition, 203; True Christian Religion, 203, 263.